To: R. N.

a gift

MW01267994

THE DECLARATION OF
DEPENDENCE

A BETRAYAL OF THE AMERICAN DREAM

A gift from
Ginger Allen

Enjoy your gift.

What People Are Saying about
The Declaration of Dependence . . .
A Betrayal of the American Dream

This One Will Challenge Your Beliefs
Jack M. Bourla, DC

If you are a status quo type person, you may want to stay away from Dr. Martingano's book, *The Declaration of Dependence*. Dr. Martingano has looked at the history of the United States and its current state of affairs and provided thought-provoking ideas on where we may have gone wrong. Unlike many others, however, he has also suggested solutions to his ideas and supported them with references throughout his book for the interested reader.

This is not a read for the timid. He challenges many of the values that Americans hold as true today and he suggests that our government is intentionally and incrementally taking away our freedoms and circumventing the Constitution. Dr. Martingano leaves no or very few stones unturned with respect to today's media and government in a way that empowers the average American in making better political decisions to ensure that we retain our freedoms.

① True; however it is an interesting point of view to explore !!!

A MUST READ! Insightful and Illuminating
Dr. Peter Kervorkian

Dr. Martingano has created an extraordinary book. It is thoroughly researched and well thought out. It is based on facts and brings to light how so many of the tenets that built the United States are slowly eroding. Sal offers clear insight as to why. The book is a must read for anyone who wants to be part of recreating the "greatness" of the American dream. A well written book, *The Declaration of Dependence* should be in the library of every American citizen.

An Eye Opening and Timely Book!
Dr. Patrick Milroy

This is an eye opening and timely book, that uncovers the truth of an American political system gone awry — a system controlled by greed, big oil, big pharma, and corrupt politicians, with the average citizen unaware and duped. What is happening in the country of my birth is shocking and we've got to stop the "oh that's just conspiracy" attitude, which this book does! Dr. Martingano's writing style is excellent, courageous, and the research that went into the book was thorough. I'd like all of my family members to challenge their understanding of U.S. politics with this book. Thank you Dr. Martingano.

Education is the key to our Freedom. A must read.
Bleeding Heart Liberal . . . Anonymous

Dr. Martingano is a clear thinker. Well done treatise of a complex subject. A great stepping stone to the subject of our Freedoms and our Country. I am a bleeding heart lifetime liberal Democrat and I agreed with this books premise and followed the logic. I would hope more people read this and become educated to the fact that there may be forces hidden from our view that just may be directing us to a submissive and less free world.

The Declaration of Dependence — Book One
The Ideas Behind the Principles for Making America Great Again

Published in the United States by Credo House Publishers,
a division of Credo Communications LLC, Grand Rapids, Michigan
credohousepublishers.com

ISBN 978-1-62586-146-7

Printed in the United States of America
First edition published 2017. Second edition 2019.

THE DECLARATION OF
DEPENDENCE

A BETRAYAL OF THE AMERICAN DREAM

DR. SAL MARTINGANO

credo
house publishers

CONTENTS

FOREWORD

Dr. Sal Martingano's book, *The Declaration of Dependence*, is a must-read book. It is hard-hitting and eye-opening, yet written in an easy-to-understand, down-to-earth style. Dr. Martingano has done the hard-lifting, researching decades of information to be able to lay out in plain sight what has been going on behind the scenes. From his family's background, being Italian immigrants leaving a failed socialist country, Dr. Martingano strips away the media's facade to reveal what is really going on. You will be awakened and challenged by reading *The Declaration of Dependence*.

William J. Federer, best-selling author

PREFACE

Americans are enamored by the story of the founding of our Constitution, as if it is a story from a good novel, yet never fully grasping the price in blood that our Constitution required. Our founding fathers left us with a sacred trust never before experienced in human history. "We the people" attempts to make sense of what has happened to this glorious country after decades of reflection on the historical events that have transformed not only the economics of this country but the terminology as well. The basis of this writing lies in the premise that *words have meaning*. Many in our society are totally unaware that when words change, so do their implications. Society in this country has been sheltered from changing terminology.

One example of changing terminology in our Constitution is in the initial intent of a *free enterprise* system of economics. Arthur C. Brooks, political commentator for the *Washington Post*, wrote an editorial column on May 23, 2010, entitled: "America Faces a New Culture War: Free enterprise vs. government control." He stated: "It is a struggle between two competing visions of the country's founding and future. In one, America will continue to be an exceptional nation organized around the principles of free enterprise—limited government, a reliance on entrepreneurship and rewards determined by market forces. In the other, America will move toward European-style statism grounded in expanding bureaucracies, a managed economy and large-scale income redistribution. These visions are not reconcilable. We must choose."[1] In today's society, free enterprise now includes governmental meddling as the basis for its survival.

America was born, in part, from the dreams of immigrants worldwide who were eager to break the ties of moral degeneracy and class distinction. These people wished to test their humanity

---

[1] *The Declaration of Dependence*

with millions of others in the competitive world of a capitalist society. Surely my grandparents had no real grasp of capitalism or what freedom really meant, coming from the socialist and pre-Fascist society of the Mussolini dictatorship in Italy. At the turn of the century, Italy was in economic ruin due to failed socialist policies and environmental challenges and it was about to worsen drastically under the ideas of Fascism, in which the individual existed only to strengthen a powerful governmental dictatorship. My grandparents and over 4 million other Italian families were willing to take the risk to escape from the land of their ancestors in an attempt to find what is inherent to the human experience: freedom. Estimations of more than 100 million Americans have at least one ancestor who came as legal immigration to the U.S. during the 1900's.

My parents, the products of immigration, were charged with building a new world for their families with the promise of relatively high wage jobs generated by industrialization and the opportunity for upward social mobility. Instead, they came face to face with the Great Depression. Survival was a matter of persistence and the clear vision that it was up to them and not some governmental regime to save them. It was World War II and the need for a change from isolationism that tested the resolve of our nation; it also effectively ended the Great Depression.

Born into the initial class of what has become the *baby boomer* generation, I grew up in a world where pride, integrity and individuality were not considered "racist" or discriminatory (as they are today) but were the keys to success. Individual success and competence, in whatever your chosen field, led to the cumulative success of society. The concept of *class distinction* did not arise from intentional, societal wrongdoing but was the motive to become a better and more productive member of society. America was known as the *land of opportunity* because class distinction was neither a deterrent to personal success nor an anchor to the social structure of society.

As a young boy I was fascinated by how things were named, and more importantly, why they were named. It took most of my elementary school years to understand why I was there. All I can remember was that school was about the memorization of facts, studying for the sake of passing exams, then just as quickly forgetting what I had learned to absorb new facts. My teachers were Masters of Teaching *what* to learn but never *how* to learn. The result was that I became a mediocre student at best and bored at worst.

There is a Buddhist proverb: when the student is ready, the teacher appears. I wasn't prepared for my teacher to appear, but the universe had other ideas. At age nine, I disobeyed my father's orders not to ride my new bicycle to a different neighborhood and promptly found myself staring at my right elbow protruding from my skin. Neighborhoods in Brooklyn, New York, in the 1950's were filled with huge maple and oak trees, left over from vast farm lands and forests of the late 1800's. I ventured into unknown territory and promptly ran my bike into a gaping hole where one of these behemoths used to stand. I bounced out of the hole but landed, out of control, on an up-slanted concrete driveway, elbow first. Oddly, the sight of my compound fractured elbow, sticking out of my skin, was less painful than the thought of what my father would do to me at the sight of the destroyed front wheel of my new bicycle. Instinctively, I jerked my right arm straight and the bone went back into the hole in my skin; I calmly walked my bike with my arm hanging at my side back to my house, prepared to face my father's wrath for my disobedience.

What followed was 11 months in a full hand to shoulder cast and I was homebound due to school safety regulations at the time. This single event started my transformation in learning with the appearance of a home schoolteacher. Suddenly, I was captive to a caring human being that was more concerned in teaching me *how* to learn rather than *what* to learn, opening my world to critical thinking at age 9. When I returned to school the next year, I found myself far ahead of my fellow students. Even the dreaded subject of history bristled with excitement. Gone were the boring days of memorization in favor of "living" the experience of learning.

I spent nearly two decades in the Boy Scout program, moving through the ranks of self-reliance until I reached assistant scoutmaster. That was where I built character and the understanding that integrity, responsibility, and knowledge are things earned and not given. Why were our standards in life being so watered down? Where were the men in my life? It was clear that our country had changed, and not in a good way. The world was getting uglier—Vietnam raged for over a decade. The respect for those who made America was being trashed in favor of an ever growing government entity that seemed to be removing our freedoms rather than protecting them. The entitlement generation was born. I finally had enough and decided to reevaluate my life.

Going through college, professors were spewing information totally foreign to me. I enrolled in a liberal arts degree program thinking it meant a general, broad-based education in which I could expand my critical thinking skills into what would eventually become my life's work. During the 1960's, I quickly found that this degree program was instituted to indoctrinate students into following the political trends and getting on board with causes because they were revolutionary to the to the American lifestyle, I was accustomed. My thinking did not lend itself to the hippie mentality of revolting against social values. Realizing my error of not being the critical thinker I thought myself to be, I changed degree programs to pursue an engineering career, specializing in architecture. Apparently, engineering was the key to the future. After one year of torture and a basic course in psychology 101, I found my tendencies were toward intuition, thoughtfulness and vitalistic thinking as opposed to analytical and the ability to think in the abstract. Leaving engineering behind I realized that my interests were in understanding complex principles and making them easy to understand. I was a teacher! Once I understood that

I can be both student and teacher, I realized that I had passed my test in critical thinking, never again dependent on what others decided to say or do.

By the 1970's, our country was experiencing shortages never before seen. Gasoline shortages because of a country called Iran? Who the hell were they? Why did a mob of young Islamic revolutionaries on November 4, 1979, overrun the U.S. Embassy in Tehran, taking more than 60 Americans hostage for 444 days? And who was the Ayatollah Khomeini? Little did I know the seeds planted in a liberal arts degree would someday be the fruit of destruction of this country.

My journey to find the real meaning of my life exploded in many directions. On one side, there were people hell-bent on change, even if they didn't know or care what that change was. On the other side were the traditional thinkers, seeking to build our country—the engineers, if you will. I found myself asking the age old question: "Who am I?"

For the next 16 years I was in heaven; I found my niche in life. Then, out of nowhere, change was yet again becoming ugly. Why was an inner NYC high school changing its curriculum to totally accommodate English as a second language? Why were academic courses being broken up into normal and remedial classes? Why were kids being talked about as if they were the "property" of a school system, speaking of them in terms of what daily attendance meant to school funding? Why did the school system have to deal with the teacher's union, rather than the teachers? Why was there a movement to dumb down our school system in general? Why was there open enrollment in colleges? I thought either you made the grade, or you didn't and what the hell is *New Math*?

Part of the answer was firmly entrenched in the actions of the 907,000 members of the American Federation of Teachers

(AFT), headed at the time by its union leader, Albert Shanker. Mr. Shanker's outward rhetoric was always tempered around better education for children. The sheer size of the union and the clout it carried through its union dues and retirement funds became the cornerstone for the progressive takeover of the educational system that led to the dramatic changes in the mid 1970's.[2]

The AFT fought for better teachers, smaller class sizes and union employee benefits that amounted to massive entitlement programs that NYC had to bear or face the wrath of a 904,000 teacher's union strike. During Shanker's presidency, teachers were no longer judged on their merit based on supervisor reviews, but by their negotiated three-year tenure rule. After three years, aside from insubordination, a teacher could not be fired. Teachers were guaranteed pay raises based on years of service rather than ability.

By 1975, NYC was in grave financial trouble and unable to meet its salary and benefit obligations to the members of the AFT. Shortly thereafter Shanker and the AFT whipped its membership into a frenzy over pay raises, benefits and the need for smaller class sizes and new teacher salary parity. NYC responded by refusing to negotiate, resulting in a five-day AFT strike shutting down of the entire NYC school system. NYC imposed an ordinance forbidding ALL city workers from striking, but Shanker called the strike anyway. As I walked the picket line, it was clear that we could be sued by the city for striking. After 5 long days, Shanker announced a settlement. Existing teachers would receive less than a 1% pay increase, stating that higher paid teachers needed to share incomes so that new teachers would receive benefits. Teachers would not be sued for striking against the city but would not be paid for days lost. Somehow this was portrayed as an equitable win for striking.

Several years later, it was discovered that Shanker and the AFT struck a deal with NYC to float a $150 million stimulus loan from

[2] http://www.uft.org/who-we-are/history/albert-shanker

the huge teacher's retirement fund for a hefty return. The five-day strike was staged to create the appearance of a show of strength by the AFT, when in fact the progressive mindset of the powerful union was not for the school children or the teachers. The strike was about building a bigger financial base for the union, sacrificing teacher salaries to bail NYC out of its financial crisis. Shanker indeed duped the teachers. In an unconfirmed Shanker quote in 1985, he may have secretly revealed his true intentions as union boss: "When schoolchildren start paying union dues, that's when I'll start representing the interests of schoolchildren."[3]

Leaving teaching and starting over to become a chiropractor with a family in tow, was the single greatest experience/ experiment of my life. I finally had the chance to find out what I was made of. In chiropractic school, I was introduced to the philosophy of life. I always tried to answer the *how* as well as the *what* in life, but I never considered the *why*. One of my initial assignments in chiropractic philosophy introduced me to the writings of Ayn Rand and a book called *The Fountainhead*. To say this was an eye-opening experience is an understatement. The author was a refugee from communist Russia to the U.S., just as my grandparents were refugees from socialist Italy. Rand used metaphors to communicate truths and lessons of life. *The Fountainhead* was about an architect, which captured my attention, since Architecture was my major in college before becoming a teacher. After reading Rand's book, I found the message was far deeper than architecture. She wrote of integrity, humanity, and freedom vs. coercion; Rand used architecture as a metaphor for the philosophy of life. I was beginning to understand the *why* in life.

What makes my writing different in this book is not in the information it contains but, in the ability, to make the "complex" easier to understand: the fruition of my life's quest. It is my intent to help empower the average American's ability to stand for what is right and not for what is expedient. Taking back our country is

---

[3] http://en.wikipedia.org/wiki/Albert_Shanker

not for the faint of heart. We are well past critical mass in terms of the damage created by years of neglect to our founding principles. If there is a collapse of the economic and political structure of this country, those that survive the inevitable rebuilding process will be totally dependent on the memory of what made this country independent.

It is my hope that my contribution will be remembered.

Once exposed to the light, you can never return to the dark.

CHAPTER ONE

MEDIA DECEPTION . . .
Fake News or Planned Agenda

S ince the beginning of time, information has been the key to development, science, and communication. In 1690, the first newspaper was published in America named *The Publick Occurrences*. By 1870, the number of newspapers published in the U.S. skyrocketed to 5,091. The age of information and news became vital to any civilized nation. Journalism became a profession created out of the rise of media. Those who chose to seek out and report news to society at large were revered as dedicated public servants not bound to any political party or faction. In fact, if you did not learn to befriend the news media or gave the impression of hiding from the public eye, your days were numbered as a public figure. Many of our presidents learned to either respect the journalist media or their longevity as a leader was in jeopardy. The early days of newspapers and what later became the *media* was truly the essence of democracy, where the will of the people played heavily in the checks and balances of politics.

With increased technology, especially television, the visual component of news was born. The media quickly learned that the power to sway a country was within their control. In just 80 years, the power of the press in reporting the news lost its luster, and the number of daily newspapers in the U.S. declined dramatically over the past half-century, according to *Editor & Publisher*, the trade journal of American newspapers. In 1950, there were just 1,772 daily newspapers and by 2008, that number dropped to 1,422 daily papers that exist today.

Historically, with three quarters of all U.S. newspapers out of business, the print media of the day was becoming irrelevant. The day of the independent journalist was slipping away. It was time to take a long, hard look at reporting the news.

By the early 2000's the transformation of the media had taken itself from news reporter, to newsmaker. Journalists quickly learned that they had to make reporting the news more visual and more Hollywood, often creating news from emotions, unsubstantiated sources or opinion editorials, rather than reporting factual content. Gone are the days of Walter Cronkite's timeless reporting of the world's most influential events including the real-time assassination of JFK. Gone is the quality reporting done by Edward R. Murrow, Chet Huntley & David Brinkley and their reporting of the Russian Sputnik. Instead of Huntley and Brinkley we got Ken and Barbie. Turn to any TV news channel; sex appeal dominates news broadcasting. News has become more agenda driven than raw news. Reporting the news and commenting on the news is quite different. One only needs to look at the fawning that took place between Obama's progressive agenda and the media and the biased distain for Trump's more apolitical, conservative agenda, to understand that the media has lost its independent perspective.

Modern media headlines often begin with openly opinionated rhetoric that sets the tone for the public before the actual news is reported. A good recent example of reporting the intended outcome of a story before it actually occurs, was the attempt by the news media to influence voters into believing that the Russians were involved in hacking the 2016 elections. Again, with the approval of former Alabama Senator Jeff Sessions, as the new Attorney General of the United States, Minnesota Democratic Senator Al Franken openly influenced the American public and media, by accusing Jeff Sessions of conspiring with the Russians at the behest of the Trump campaign, before Trump's invocation. Buried in the media reporting of the accusation, is the admittance from the House Intelligence Chairman, Devin Nunez, the Director of National Intelligence, James Clapper, the CIA and the FBI, that "that is absolutely no proof or evidence of any kind of Russian collusion or Russian hacking into the U.S. electoral process nor what was actually hacked," yet the media ran with the story as if guilty before proven innocent. To the low information voter, who usually reads the first few sentences of a story, all they see is "Russian hacking." This, in my opinion, is a deliberate attempt to distort the facts of a story to fit an agenda and is totally inconsistent with proper news vetting.

When news becomes biased, opinionated or agenda driven, full news coverage is impossible. In the past, the media could easily influence public thought, put political leaders on the defensive or take out political figures, using first amendment protection. Our present administration has "stuck a pencil in the eye of the media," by not being influenced via slanted or agenda driven reporting. Modern social media outlets like Twitter, Instagram, etc., can instantly bypass the whims of the media. Never in the history of news reporting, has the media been so challenged as we are witnessing today.

To the unengaged population, the visual impact of what new media "talking heads" have to say, often overshadows the truth. News channels now are carbon copies of each other, with key words being repeated over and over. Gone are the hard-hitting questions and unbiased reporting. Even the timeless Larry King faithfully followed the charade of asking "soft ball" questions to pre-scripted answers, if it met the agenda of the topic material.

Media Reference

ᴷᵉᵉᵖ mind that media outlets are supported by advertising dollars and by elite controlling Foundations like the Rockefeller Foundation, who set the news agenda behind the scenes.[4] This presents a unique challenge for both the news outlets and the public. TV and newspaper outlets used to have a monopoly on news coverage; however, differing opinions brought to public's attention via social media, have challenged the status quo. As a result, TV news outlets have gone to Hollywood style production sets and slick marketing to overcome the social media presence and hold viewer's attention. Similarities can be drawn to the taxi cab industry's challenge with Uber. Uber has set the taxi industry reeling with better, personalized service at a price far less than traditional taxi service. No longer is there a monopoly or need for expensive state government controlled taxi medallions (up to a million dollars each), allowing taxi medallion prices to plummet to all-time lows.[5] In the process, some independent Uber drivers are on the receiving end of violent acts of car sabotage. Social media and Uber have changed the way business is conducted that favor the public to the chagrin of the formerly unchallenged elites.

For the news media, they are faced with creative ways of making the news rather than reporting it. Controversy is what keeps the public engaged. For the public, they are now faced with the prospects of deciding what is fake, agenda driven news and what is genuine. Thanks to the candidacy of a non-political presidential candidate, who will not "go along to get along," the influence of the media on public opinion is severely challenged. It's no secret that the news media appears to have an overwhelmingly liberal bias; but what does that actually mean? When taking a critical look at news outlets, it's important to understand historical perspective. There is a major difference between opinionated or agenda driven news, as it relates to liberal vs. conservative views. The premise of this book is that *"words have meaning"* and without

[4] https://www.rockefellerfoundation.org/about-us/news-media
[5] http://www.usatoday.com/story/news/2015/05/17/taxi-medallion-values-decline-uber-rideshare/27314735

understanding the political, social and economic terminology, it's very easy to get lost in the hype rather than the content.[6]

To put this discussion into perspective, let's understand that all is not what it appears to be. There is a hierarchy or chain of command in every corporation; no surprise therefore, that the news media is owned by multiple layers of corporations. Things tend to get murky, as they relate to the media, when names like the Bilderberg Group, the Council on Foreign Relations or the Trilateral Commission enter the conversation. Either people will simply ignore the reference or experience a gut-wrenching tremor, since "conspiracy theory" is readily associated with these organizations. The fact is the Bilderberg Group, for example, meets every year in private, with its 120 or so powerful and influential heads of state, corporations and banking members to discuss world policy, including how the media puts out their message. George Soros is a long-standing member, so it's also no surprise we hear his name bantered about in present day media and politics.[7]

To be more specific, media outlets back in the 1980's, were owned by some 50 media companies/corporations. Today, thanks to mergers and outright takeovers, the entire news media is controlled by six major media giants, (GE, News-corp, Disney, Viacom, Time Warner and CBS) which control 90% of what we read, watch or listen to, all designed to give the illusion of choice. To the astute observer, this consolidation and control over news media coverage is readily seen on TV news outlets like: CNN, CNBC, ABC, NBC, MSNBC and others, in that they all have similar attractive "talking heads," appearing on similar sets with similar colored moving graphics, that essentially report the same news. To be honest, modern new coverage has come a long way from the days of Walter Cronkite's monotone voice or the dry presentations of The Huntly Brinkley Report, with nothing more than a bland backdrop and a clock but nonetheless we must separate marketing from news reporting.

[6] *https://www.quora.com/Why-is-are-network-media-personnel-overwhelmingly-liberal*
[7] *http://www.businessinsider.com/this-chart-shows-the-bilderberg-groups-connection-to-everything-in-the-world-2012-6*

There are well over 200 media executives that literally control all the content of the news we see every day. Information overload is part of the plan, since most people tend to shut down, shut up and become complacent when faced with conflicting stories, presented in rapid succession. Media now dominates 1 out or every 5 hours of television. Print media is dominated by the "Wall Street Journal" in America, "The Sun" in Europe and "The Australian" in the land down under. Newspapers have disappeared exponentially with the rise of social media outlets like Google, MSN and the multitude of privately-owned web news outlets. Corporate media control of radio is no different. 80% of all radio station programming have matching playlists, from music to news. The result of all these mergers, corporate control over news content and the ever-growing challenges of visual marketing appeal, has led to a polarization toward liberal, democratic ideologies.[8] Over the past 100 years the Democratic liberal wing of the both the U.S. Senate and the House, has held power nearly twice as long as the more conservative wing of the Republican Party, including the White House.[9]

In May 1985, Australian publisher Rupert Murdoch announced that he and American industrialist Marvin Davis intended to develop "a network of independent stations" to compete directly with CBS, NBC and ABC. Around the same time, the political voice of "Conservative Talk Radio" was being heard in Sacramento, California, with the Rush Limbaugh show. By 1988, is was clear that conservative talk radio, under Limbaugh, had finally come of age, as a counterbalance to the liberal dominated TV news media. It was only a matter of time before other conservative voices like Sean Hannity, Herman Cain, Glen Beck, Mark Levin and others joined in spreading the conservative voice in America.

In 1996, Murdoch asked former Republican Party political strategist Roger Ailes, to start the Fox News Channel and a new chapter in competitive news media reporting was born. Combined with the growing listenership of Conservative Talk Radio, the

---

[8] *http://www.businessinsider.com/these-6-corporations-control-90-of-the-media-in-america-2012-6*
[9] *https://en.wikipedia.org/wiki/Political_power_in_the_United_States_over_time#Party_Control_of_Congress*

Fox News Channel presented the first real challenge to liberal dominated, national news corporations. The silent millions of people, stymied by a lack of ideological diversity, suddenly had a voice and the ideological "war" had begun. The Fox News Channel made no pretense of promoting conservative political positions. Critics of the Fox News Channel have stated: "Fox News has a bias favoring the political right and the Republican Party," Fox News host Chris Wallace stated, "I think we are the counter-weight to NBC News . . . they have a liberal agenda, and we tell the other side of the story."[10]

The Effects of Shrinking News Outlets

Aside from the obvious superior marketing appeal TV news now has, key news factors or being lost. Net Neutrality is at stake when media mergers occur. Net neutrality involves a lack of restrictions on content on the internet, however, with big businesses supporting campaigns financially, they tend to have influence over political news issues. These big businesses that also have control over internet usage or the airwaves could possibly make the content biased from their political standpoint or they could restrict usage for conflicting political views, therefore eliminating Net Neutrality.

An oligopoly is when a few corporate firms dominate a marketplace. When large scale media companies buy out the smaller-scaled media companies, they become more powerful within that market. As large media firms continue to eliminate their business competition through buyouts or forcing them out (because they lack the resources or finances) the remaining companies dominate the media industry and create a media oligopoly.[11]

---

[10] *https://en.wikipedia.org/wiki/Fox_News*
[11] *https://en.wikipedia.org/wiki/Concentration_of_media_ownership*

Diversity of Viewpoints

It is important to elaborate upon the issue of media consolidation and its effect upon the diversity of information reaching the public. Critics of consolidation raise the issue of whether monopolistic or oligopolistic control of a local media market can be fully accountable and dependable in serving unbiased information the public. Depending on your political slant, one can make the case for media bias. The most widely watched channel these days is Fox News, which has amassed a larger volume of viewers than does NBC or CBS or ABC news. So, it's hard to make the argument that network news or "mainstream media" is mostly liberal when the network leader is a news source that leans to the right of the political spectrum. The argument, therefore, should not be about media bias favoring the one political ideology or another but rather what "elite" agenda is appropriate at the time.

During the Obama administration, media coverage favored the liberal agenda, since the foreseeable future was another democrat dominated administration. Hillary was to be the next media darling, which suited the status quo of mainstream media. The republicans were on the defensive and resorted to the same media tactics of the democrats. Fox news was ablaze, pointing out the agenda of the Clinton Foundation, where huge sums of donations poured into the Hillary campaign via their foundation, in what appeared to be a "pay for play" opportunity for supportive corporate interests. The mainstream media remained generally silent. When the planes of then, Attorney Loretta Lynch met with Bill Clinton on the tarmac in Phoenix, to discuss golf and the grandchildren, just prior to Hillary's congressional hearing on her email scandal, the mainstream media, except for Fox News, again remained generally silent. Conservative outrage erupted when days later FBI director James Comey announced that Hillary's indiscretions over top secret government residing on her private server, did not meet prosecutorial standards. Mainstream media is still nursing its black eye for that one, depending on "plausible deniability" rather than factual news reporting.

The Conservative Daily Post is the counterbalance to Politico. Both publications specialize in creating "fake news," whether intentionally or otherwise. Both publications rely on bloggers that hyperventilate political stories that favor their reader's political views. In itself, both publications have the right to speak (or write) what they want under First Amendment protection, but both are guilty of fake news. Politico partners with mainstream news organizations like CBS and NBC, while The Conservative Daily Post takes in content from many sources but focusses on stories that invoke visceral responses.[12] Surely, political slants are part of the equation for all media outlets, that's why we have choices in America. If you don't like what you see on TV . . . change the channel. The motives of mainstream news media coverage is readership, viewership and advertising dollars.

Freedom of the Press and Editorial Independence

Very often network heads refuse to print or air stories that run contrary to their base. Past examples would be the repeated refusal of networks to air "ads" from anti-war advocates to liberal groups like MoveOn.org, or religious groups like the United Church of Christ, regardless of factual basis. Journalists may be directly sponsored by parties who they write for, slanting the subject of their journalism to favor their sponsors' opinion. Consequently, if the companies dominating a media market choose to suppress stories that do not serve their interests, the public suffers.

The First Amendment to the U.S. Constitution was to encourage a free press. It was Thomas Jefferson who said, "The only security of all is in a free press. The force of public opinion cannot be resisted when permitted freely to be expressed. The agitation

---

[12] http://www.msn.com/en-us/news/us/this-beauty-queen-was-the-face-of-a-fake-news-website-she-says-she-had-no-idea/ar-AAnHZtH?li=BBnb7Kz
[13] https://keepthewaterspure.wordpress.com

it produces must be submitted to. It is necessary, to keep the waters pure."[13] Freedom of the press has become a contentious issue, since 'freedom' doesn't necessarily imply truth.

The senseless shooting at schools and theaters has left the anti-constitutionalists, frothing at the mouth to rid this nation of its 2nd amendment. Gun control became the talking point for every news station. Nearly every news channel now begins with "an agenda" story or two of a shooting somewhere in the country, mostly void of any balanced reporting from the media. Fast forward to present day news reporting from Australia, which enacted the strictest gun confiscation laws in the world several years ago. The first-year results are now in: Australia-wide, homicides are up 3.2 percent; Australia-wide, assaults are up 8.6 percent; Australia-wide, armed robberies are up 44 percent (yes, 44 percent!). In the state of Victoria alone, homicides with firearms are now up 300 percent.[14] Note that while the law-abiding citizens turned them in, the criminals did not, and criminals still possess their guns! Loss of liberty equals loss of life. If the media in this country continues to push administrative agendas rather than reporting unbiased on the news, journalism is dead.

Keep in mind the media in general is big business requiring sponsors. The media can be bought and sold to the highest bidder. The events in Benghazi, Libya, on Sept 11, 2012, demonstrated incredible media bias. At the "hearings" where the truth was to be revealed, not a single news channel asked the hard questions of how this attack could have happened; nor did they ask why five days of misinformation was spewed daily while just one day after the event, Libya's president confirmed the attack was not spontaneous but an Al-Qaeda terrorist attack. Later testimony from the then CIA deputy director Mike Morell revealed that he was briefed on what was about to happen the day before the attack in Benghazi from first-hand reports from within the Libyan embassy itself but chose instead to rely on his CIA advisors in Langley, Virginia.[15] More

[14] http://www.snopes.com/crime/statistics/ausguns.asp#4cq2VHopUVetKRzJ.99
[15] http://www.washingtontimes.com/news/2014/apr/2/cia-leader-morell-denies-role-benghazi-cover-up

importantly was the cover-up when Mr. Morell admitted changing the storyline to the press, supposedly not to inflame any further attacks, by leaving out key phrases (like the attack was initiated by Islamic Terrorists). Instead, he continued the spontaneous protest storyline sparked by an obscure YouTube movie.[16]

Similarly, media bias changed the course of history by simply putting out false information on whomever they didn't support. Examples of media bias are: the destruction of Governor Sarah Palin by false accusations, climate-gate, guns are evil, Senator Edward Kennedy's Chappaquiddick (where a young woman's death literally got swept under the media's rug), and the media's apparent indifference toward reporting all that is known about President Obama prior to his election, as required by the constitution.

More recently, the Obama friendly news media carried on the traditions of selective reporting by minimizing the 2010 FBI's seizure of personal emails from journalist, James Rosen, without a warrant,[17] the National Security Administration's (NSA) spying on millions of unsuspecting American citizens,[18] or the many blocked attempts by journalists to investigate controversial stories via requests under the Freedom of Information Act, by the Obama administration.[19]

Media is at war over words not substance. Media reports civil disobedience as our first amendment rights. . . . No dialogue just relentless organized civil disobedience disguised as right to protest.

So strong has the influence of the media been, that it can shape political outcomes. The progressive democratic agenda along with a complicit media, sees to it that the public sees only what they need to see and hear. The inauguration of Obama's second term left the Republican Party with an approval rating of only 16% partially because of media bias. The Republican Party in turn, became the party of lying low and cajoling to the democrats for fear of further

---

[16] http://pjmedia.com/tatler/2014/04/02/did-cias-mike-morell-lie-under-oath-about-changing-the-benghazi-talking-points
[17] http://www.huffingtonpost.com/news/james-rosen
[18] https://www.eff.org/deeplinks/2013/06/confirmed-nsa-spying-millions-americans
[19] http://www.pbs.org/newshour/rundown/obama-administration-sets-new-record-withholding-foia-requests

bad press. How can the media, disguised as unbiased journalism, have such power of persuasion? It is as if the media has become an actual 3rd political party, while giving the appearance of neutrality.

Politics is power, whereas the media has to maintain an apolitical stance. The media has demonstrated anything but an apolitical stance. Presidential elections are won or lost in the court of public opinion. However, there have been four presidential elections where the candidate has won the popular vote but lost the election.[20] Public opinion is shaped by what people hear and see. Before modern media, people often never saw their presidential candidates, depending only on word of mouth and newsprint. Today, candidates raise millions of dollars to be seen and heard in the media, leading to coverage on the "highest bidder." The visual appeal of a candidate can be destroyed by scandal, whether the scandal is real or contrived.

In 2013, Republican Governor Chris Christie of New Jersey was the target of a media frenzy over alleged political maneuvering. Christie was alleged to have intentionally shut down one lane of the George Washington Bridge in Ft. Lee, New Jersey, for four days as retribution against the town's mayor for declining to endorse Christie in the last re-election. As a result a special committee was created by the New Jersey Assembly and was given subpoena powers, appointing former federal prosecutor Reid Schar to serve as special counsel.[21] In the Christie case, media coverage was enormous. Every news channel, newspaper and media personality covered the airwaves over this relatively insignificant event. A closer look at this event finds cause to question the media's intent. Republican Chris Christie was a leading presidential candidate for the Republican Party. The leading candidate for the Democratic Party is former Secretary of State and former first lady Hillary Clinton.

The way the media covered republican Chris Christy vs. how the media covered Democrat Hillary Clinton was astounding.

[20] http://www.infoplease.com/spot/campaign2000race.html
[21] http://www.washingtonpost.com/politics/transcript-chris-christies-news-conference-on-george-washington-bridge-scandal/2014/01/09/d0f4711c-7944-11e3-8963-b4b654bcc9b2_story.html

The disproportionate media coverage of a lane closure on a busy bridge to that of the killing of the American ambassador in Benghazi and three others clearly demonstrates media's willingness toward a biased agenda. Sadly, the public misses the political implications, being led to believe that the killing of American diplomats on foreign soil as well as the subsequent lies told by the executive government officials as cover-up is of little consequence when compared to a traffic jam on a bridge in a local city in New Jersey.

The same is true about the Clinton/Trump coverage. Clinton was caught with a private email server in her house containing classified documents, verified to have been hacked due to lack of any government security measures. The media played the incident down to an oversight having little or no consequence to American security. Trump was accused of coercion with the Russians to disrupt the presidential elections, plus having diplomatic discussions with Russian officials, with the intent of furthering his business empire. The media used a document with unnamed sources to make the case for Trumps guilt, even though government officials stated that there is absolutely no proof of any collusion.

The intent of this discussion is not to report the "he said, she said" aspect of media coverage but to point out the hypocrisy that "all is not what it appears to be." Further, with respect to the Trump/Russian connection, perhaps the media was duped by the Democrats as well. Clear photographic evidence exists demonstrating that top Kremlin officials like the Russian Ambassador Sergey Kislyak met with Democrats Chuck Shummer and Nancy Pelosi numerous times before the 2016 presidential campaign. The Obama white house was sponsor to other Russian dignitaries and lobbyists more than 20 times during his administration. Perhaps the initial leaked document to the press, by the Democrats, was designed to blame Trump for the exact deeds committed by the democrats thus allowing "fake news" to become the focus of public attention.[22]

---

[22] *http://www.lifezette.com/polizette/trump-roasts-pelosi-schumer-russian-hypocrisy*

Politics has become an exercise in military tactics. The military of all countries rely on stealth and deception to win conflicts. There are 32 news media outlets (armies) in the U.S., all but 6 are of liberal mindset. To win political wars, oftentimes several "fake" plans are leaked intentionally, in hopes that the opposing forces fall for the deception, while the real plan is initiated behind the scenes. The mainstream media has become the "whipping post" for both political parties, depending on which is in power. Fake news becomes the deception tactic while the controllers (corporations) of the media exercise their real plan. The population of the U.S., and the power granted to them under the constitution, are the spoils of political warfare. Politicians are no longer the employees of the people but instead the ranking officers of political warfare, taking their marching order from the corporate and elite generals who oversee the political landscape for power and wealth.

Despite the best efforts of the media and the political elites, there is an occasional disruption of plans. History has shown that the power of the media and the resources of political parties eventually encompasses all individuals (politicians) that enter politics. Strategic alliance abound, delicately intertwined so that the politician can never stand alone. It has been said that we have one political party posing as two for the purpose of allowing the public a sense of authority and control. History is replete with alternate political parties gaining control over the country with similar rhetoric year after year yet accomplishing little of their intended goals. The reason may be that a politician's first allegiance is to fulfill the objectives of his ideology (corporate sponsor) and not the will of the people he represents. Politicians that defy their obligations to those seeking payback for their support, soon find themselves embellished in scandal or face the wrath of a compliant news media.

The election of Donald Trump set politics and the news industry reeling. "Swamp" politicians find themselves with no alliances to Trump. How could this outsider, this TV personality slip past their defenses? The very best efforts of the corporate elites, the dutiful efforts by a compliant media, the lack of insider political support and every political poll in American had gotten it wrong. The reason for Trumps victory over the establishment, including the massive Clinton political machine, was the fact that Trump touched the inner soul of a formerly compliant citizenry. The people realized, that Trump had no political ties or alliances with Washington. Trump was a consummate businessman with a no nonsense attitude toward success. Trump was not intimidated by "empty suits" that speak with eloquence but proceed with agendas. Despite 18 legitimate republican candidates speaking party rhetoric, Trump touched the souls of common sense. The population was energized by a massive surge of realism that they had not seen in their lifetime.

It made no difference that Trump didn't have any real political experience; for that matter neither did Obama. For the first time in memory, a presidential candidate was speaking the language that people understood, which made mainstream media coverage less relevant. People realized that the media was not happy with Trumps popularity by their continual attacks on everything Trump did, some of which became humorous. Courage and the ability to stand on one's principles is not a strong point in politics. One can compromise within one's principles but should never compromise on one's principles. Obvious media bias broke the rules on principles every day, only raising the courage of the silent masses that yearned for the return of common-sense principles. In the end, it is this author's opinion that the mainstream media did more to help Trump, despite the appearance of attacking him. The lessons to be learned is to not underestimate the will of the people and that media bias is a double-edged sword.

This is the time to make a stand. The Republican Party, specifically the conservative minds of this country, has absolutely nothing to lose by standing on principles. The proverbial media bully has met its match under the new administration. It's time to "man up" and level the political playing field. Pretty faces and universal talking points rather than neutral reporting and unbiased journalism had successfully convinced the low-information citizen that the progressive movement is in their best interest; something akin to journalistic malpractice. My point is not about political parties, it is about exposing the journalistic fraud.

"We have nothing to fear but fear itself," the famous words of FDR in 1932 were to remind Americans that the nation's common difficulties concerned only material things. Media bias has become a driving force that should never be, resorting to a war with words rather than substance. "**F**alse **E**vidence **A**ppearing **R**eal" is the acronym for "fear;" only those with vision and experience can fight off the paralyzing effect of fear. It is my hope that we do not allow actors reporting so-called news on national TV, to be seen as experts, let alone control a nation's destiny.

For Further Reading

Answers Corporation. "How Many US Senators and Congressmen Are Conviced Felons?" WikiAnswers. http://wiki. answers.com/Q/How_many_US_senators_and_congressmen_ are_convicted_felons (accessed July 17, 2014).

Benson, Bill, and M. J. Beckman. The law that never was: the fraud of the 16th Amendment and personal income tax. South Holland, IL (Box 550, South Holland 60473): Constitutional Research Assoc., 1985.

"COMMON CORE." COMMON CORE. http://whatiscommoncore. wordpress.com/ (accessed July 16, 2014).

Sothern, Marci. "Responsibilities of the Federal Government." eHow. http://www.ehow.com/list_7654222_responsibilities-federal-government.html#ixzz2wE9vPYin (accessed July 16, 2014).

Wikimedia Foundation. "Patriot Act." Wikipedia. http:// en.wikipedia.org/wiki/Patriot_Act (accessed July 16, 2014).

YouTube. "Gun Myths Gone in Five Minutes: ABC News 20/20." YouTube. https://www.youtube.com/watch?v=682JLrsUmEM (accessed July 17, 2014).

Zieve, Sher. "Behind Common Core: Forcing Marxism/Nazism on America's Children." GulagBoundcom. http://gulagbound. com/38714/common-core-forcing-marxismnazism-on-americas-children/ (accessed July 16, 2014).

CHAPTER TWO

INFORMATION OVERLOAD OR INDIFFERENCE

I t was evident early in the research for this book, that there would be no beginning or ending for topics; it is a "snap shot" glimpse of our continued political and philosophical destruction as a country. At times it appears that we are in the studio audience of a bad sitcom. Other times we are faced with the brutal realities of an out-of-control government.

My intent is to present many of the iconic newsworthy topics that often fall within the parameters of political scandals, in a reader-friendly format. How many times are we faced with confusing journalism, filled with emotion yet lacking substance? News is meant to be reported in an unbiased manner, unencumbered by political motivation or agenda-driven rhetoric. Sadly, journalism has become an entertainment-driven ratings game where the lines of truth are often blurred beyond recognition. The result is information overload in which "we the people" no longer participate. Never have I seen such indifference to the facts. As a student of history, I continually ask myself, "is this what really happened"? The answer often cannot be found by web searches but by understanding political agendas—it is here that my quest began.

The Cost of Political Business

The American government is abusing its power in ways that would infuriate the colonists, yet we sit idly by and let the government reign their tyranny on top of us.[23] Alexander Hamilton noted, "when government obtains the ability to vote themselves power and money, that will be the downfall of this country." Hamilton's statement concerning government's ability to vote themselves power and money has come to fruition over the last decade where compensation of federal employees has risen faster than compensation of private-sector employees. Therefore, the average federal civilian worker now earns 74 percent more in wages and benefits than the average worker in the U.S. private sector.[24]

Hamilton was specific in pointing out that: "A fondness for power is implanted, in most men, and it is natural to abuse it, when acquired." After years of public service, Hamilton clearly understood that: 'you believe the government is there to protect you yet I would argue that it is now the single biggest threat to your well-being, I worry more about what the government is going to do to thwart my liberty and freedoms.' Since Hamilton's era, government has continued to be the biggest threat to individual liberty and freedom. History has had no chance to repeat itself since Hamilton made his statement; this simple fact has always been.

As the non-government worker clocks in 40 - 80 hours a week, President Obama activated a 1% pay raise for all 4.4 million government workers, by way of executive order.[25] 4.4 million Federal employees are receiving an across-the-board pay raise in addition to a 2% increase implemented in January 2010.[26]

For the fifth year in a row, lawmakers voted not to reject their automatic cost of living raise that will increase the annual salary of members by $3,400 to a total of $158,103 per year. In an article published on the Fox News website, Dick Morris writes: "Members of Congress worked only 103 days in 2013 and have the only job in the country whose occupants can set their own salary without

[23] http://ibankcoin.com/americantyranny/a-day-that-56-men-declared-our- independence-from-tyranny-time-to-do-it-again
[24] http://www.downsizinggovernment.org/overpaid-federal-workers
[25] http://www.zerohedge.com/news/2013-12-24/president-obamas-executive- order-raises-government-worker-salaries-1
[26] http://www.downsizinggovernment.org/overpaid-federal-workers

regard to performance, profit, or economic climate."[27] It goes to show how out of touch with reality politicians can be. They forget that their salaries are paid by taxpayers. Average American citizens are being forced to tighten their belts, that is if they even have a job, yet members of Congress will have an extra $3,400 to do with as they please."[28]

The facts are found in the underreported retirement benefits of Congress and their political leaders:

Salary of retired U.S. Presidents: $450,000/year for life Salary of Speaker of the House: $223,500/year for life

Compare those numbers with salaries of military personnel; their average salary when deployed is $38,000. The average income of a full commissioned officer with combat experience and full training toward the safety and security of our country, receives 50% of their salary rate at retirement, or approximately $46,156/year for life.[29]

In 2012, federal workers had an average wage of $81,704, according to data from the U.S. Bureau of Economic Analysis. By comparison, the average wage of the nation's 104 million private-sector workers was $54,995. When benefits such as health care and pensions are included, the federal compensation over private workers is even larger.[30] In 2012, federal worker compensation averaged $114,976, with the private sector averaging $65,917.

When people become indifferent to the news and even lose interest in their constitutional responsibilities, the loss of freedom is inevitable. Historically, democracies do not often exceed 200 years; the reason is that a democracy is a form of government founded on the principle of either elected individuals representing the people (as is the government of the United States) or as a direct democracy, where the people

---

[27] http://www.foxnews.com/story/2007/06/23/do-nothing-congress-mdash- big-salary-little-work-free-trips
[28] http://usgovinfo.about.com/cs/agencies/a/raise4congress.htm
[29] http://usmilitary.about.com/cs/joiningup/a/recruiter5.htm
[30] http://www.fedsmith.com/2012/03/25/average-federal-salary-lowest- average-pay

themselves are responsible for making all decisions.[31] The success of a democracy is dependent on the willingness of the people to remain involved and accountable for their decisions.

Our country was founded on constitutional principles to ensure freedom from a controlling centralized government. The U.S. Constitution is a limitation on government through the separation of powers via independent branches of government, all designed to protect American citizens from tyranny. Fifteen years after the signing of the

U.S. Constitution, it was deemed necessary to further delineate rights that were "unalienable": rights given to us by our Creator rather than by government.[32] Through the efforts of Thomas Jefferson and James Madison, a constitutional convention of states was formed to add a *Bill of Rights* to the Constitution.

On December 15, 1791, the first 10 Amendments to the Constitution, known as the *Bill of Rights*, were ratified by congress. The Constitution's first three words, "We the People," emphasize rule by the people—not a king or a dictator, not the president, Supreme Court justices, members of Congress or state legislators. Foremost in the minds of our founding fathers was the First Amendment to the United States Constitution.

"Congress shall make no law respecting an establishment of religion, or prohibiting the free exercise thereof; or abridging the freedom of speech, or of the press; or the right of the people peaceably to assemble, and to petition the Government for a redress of grievances."[33]

So important is the ability of the citizens to remain above reproach by a controlling government, that freedom of speech, the press and peaceful assembly was uniquely specified by our founding fathers.[34]

---

[31] http://en.wikipedia.org/wiki/Direct democracy
[32] http://www.breitbart.com/Big- Government/2013/09/23/What-Did- Thomas-Jefferson-Mean-By-Unalienable-Rights
[33] http://constitutioncenter.org/constitution/preamble/preamble
[34] http://en.wikipedia.org/wiki/First A mendment to the United States Constitution

FDR's New Deal and LBJ's Great Society were experiments in "social engineering," attempting to reshape the behavior of the poor and lower class on welfare rolls and into grand middle class. The attitude was that "we are all in this together" and as such we should be equal in its successes and failures. The ultimate failures of both these progressive centralized governmental experiments was that it was an experimental driven engineering project which had never sought the support or even the acquiescence of popular majorities. In fact, the most notable outcome of progressive ideologies is the expansion of entitlement programs to artificially support what their political theories have failed to produce.[35]

Under the presidency of Woodrow Wilson, the progressive political movement took hold. In 1913, Wilson ran on a platform of social reform arguing that a strong centralized government was necessary to fight for anti-trust legislation and labor rights with his "New Freedom" initiative.[36] However, his policies became nothing more than "regulated monopolies," co-opted by special business interests leading to the passage of the 16th Amendment of the U.S. Constitution, which allowed the Congress to levy an income tax without the approval of individual states. This income tax was done to support ever increasing centralized federal government programs.

Soon after the ratification of the 16th Amendment, Congress levied a 1 percent tax on personal incomes greater than $3,000 and a 6 percent tax on incomes above $500,000. These taxes affect only a very small proportion of the population. Later in 1913, In Stratton's Independence v. Howbert, the Supreme Court redefines income under the tax law as the "gain derived from capital, from labor, or from both combined." Few realize that the original intent of the tax code was to levy taxes on "earnings" from income and not the income itself.[37] Changing the tax code was an attempt to drain the wealth of the nation under the guise that it was necessary to finance the costs of World War I. To be certain,

[35] http://www.heritage.org/research/reports/2007/07/the-progressive-movement- and-the-transformation-of-american-politics
[36] http://www.shmoop.com/progressive-era-politics/woodrow-wilson.html
[37] http://www.annenbergclassroom.org/Files/Documents/Books/Our%20Constitution/Sixteenth%20Amendment Our%20 Constitution.pdf

the conclusion of World War I did not reinstate the original intent of the tax code but only served as a progressive ploy to control the wealth of the American population legally.

The Fraud of the 16th Amendment

The intrigue and deception regarding the 16th Amendment continued but was never publicly reported by the press. Outgoing Secretary of State for the Taft administration and probable incoming advisor to the Wilson administration, Philander Knox, committed fraud when he declared the 16th Amendment officially ratified.[38] "There were 48 states at that time, and three-fourths, or 36, of them were required to give their approval for the 16th Amendment to be ratified. The process took almost the whole term of the Taft administration, from 1909 to 1913.

Knox had received responses from only 42 states when he declared the 16th amendment ratified on February 25, 1913, under pressure by the Wilson administration to have his signature bill (The 16th Amendment tax code) ratified. Knox acknowledged that four of those states (Utah, Conn, R.I. and N.H.) had rejected it, bringing the count to 38, while Kentucky and Oklahoma had not responded bringing the count to 36. The state constitution of Tennessee prohibited its state legislature from acting on any proposed amendment to the U.S. Constitution sent by Congress until after the next election of state legislators, which dropped the count to 35, one less than that necessary for ratification at the time Wilson announced its ratification. By the final count less than 20 of the required 36 states had ratified the 16th Amendment. Many attempts have been made to repeal the 16th Amendment under grounds that it did not adhere to Constitutional law, but all have failed. If one allows the selective dismissal of the law, those that allow it must be held accountable.

President Wilson knew that for the progressive movement to fundamentally change the rule of law under the Constitution, he must convince the citizens of the U.S. that the *Bill of Rights,* especially the 1st Amendment, could become a detriment

---

[38] *http://www.givemeliberty.org/features/taxes/notratified.htm*

to national security. While the Progressives differed in their assessment of the problems and how to resolve them, they believed that government at every level must be actively involved in these reforms. The existing constitutional system was outdated and must be made into a dynamic, evolving instrument of social change, aided by scientific knowledge and shared journalistic reviews. In short, Constitutional law is to be enforced on the citizens but not on its elected officials.

President Wilson set his sights on breaking the 1st Amendment, especially the freedom of the press. He did so by "cozying" up to the independent media by having dinners at the White House, inviting key journalists and newspaper owners under the guise of "cooperation and transparency," when in fact, the motive was to gain influence into what was being reported to the world.

Four decades later in another landmark progressive case: *New York Times Co. v. United States* (1971), in which the administration of President Richard Nixon sought to ban the publication of the Pentagon Papers (classified government documents about the Vietnam War secretly copied and reported by *The New York Times* analyst, Daniel Ellsberg). These documents revealed that the U.S. had secretly enlarged the scale of the Vietnam War with the bombings of nearby Cambodia and Laos along with the extermination of the North Vietnam village of My Lai, where military intelligence failed to confirm the presence of Vietcong resulting in the slaughter of hundreds of innocent men, women and children. None of this was reported in the mainstream media. Daniel Ellsberg was charged with conspiracy, espionage and theft of government property, but the charges were later dropped after prosecutors investigating the Watergate Scandal soon discovered that the Nixon Administration had ordered the so-called White House Plumbers to engage in unlawful efforts to discredit Ellsberg.[39]

First Amendment rights have been put to the test once again in 2013 with the case of Edward Snowden and the National Security Council (NSA). Snowden will go down in history as one of

[39] *http://en.wikipedia.org/wiki/Pentagon_Papers*

America's most consequential whistleblowers, alongside Daniel Ellsberg. He is responsible for handing over material from one of the world's most secretive government organizations; the NSA. In a note accompanying the first set of documents Snowden provided, he wrote: "I understand that I will be made to suffer for my actions," but despite Snowden's determination to be publicly unveiled, he repeatedly insisted that he wants to avoid the media spotlight. "I don't want public attention because I don't want the story to be about me. I want it to be about what the US government is doing." He also said, "I have no intention of hiding who I am because I know I have done nothing wrong..." and "I know the government will demonize me." It was then, he said, that he "watched as Obama advanced the very policies that I thought would be reined in," and as a result, "I got hardened." He learned just how all-consuming the NSA's surveillance activities were, claiming "they are intent on making every conversation and every form of behavior in the world known to them." Once Snowden reached the conclusion that the NSA's surveillance net would soon be irrevocable, he said it was just a matter of time before he chose to act. "What they're doing poses an existential threat to democracy." For Snowden, it is a matter of principle: "The government has granted itself power it is not entitled to. There is no public oversight." "I carefully evaluated every single document I disclosed to ensure that each was legitimately in the public interest, he said. There are all sorts of documents that would have made a big impact that I didn't turn over, because harming people isn't my goal. Transparency is." [40]

It is important to note that the above information is meant only to disclose the slow, insidious infiltration of the progressive movement onto the dismantling of our Constitutional Bill of Rights. Freedom of the press gave unprecedented uniqueness to the transparency of the United States. However, in 2014, under the Obama administration, the U.S. has fallen to 46th according to The World for Press Freedom. [41]

---

[40] h202 http://www.theguardian.com/world/2013/jun/09/edward-snowden-nsa- whistleblower-surveillance
[41] http://townhall.com/tipsheet/katiepavlich/2014/02/18/united-states-falls- to-46th-in-the-world-for-press-freedom-n1796607

Will the citizens of the U.S. view the acts of Ellsberg and Snowden as treason against the United States or as heroes for attempting to uphold the very Constitutional laws elected, and appointed U.S. government officials have chosen to ignore? It is important to realize that Freedom is nothing more than an illusion without diligent review.

Politics is a game of chess, where one must plan several moves ahead in order to achieve victory. Confusion leads to a lack of planning and an eventual lack of interest in what is happening around them. So, it is with the pace of recent political scandals where progressive ideologies often go unrecognized leading to the eventual loss of constitutional respect.

Every president since Ronald Reagan, not including President Trump, has moved this country deeper into the abyss of political chaos and financial disaster. Political parties have become nothing more than one party posing as two, keeping us amused as in a shell game where we continually guess where the prize is located. The idea of a balanced budget has become a "racist" ideology because of its implication favoring the people that keep this country prosperous against those depending on entitlements. It appears that our entire culture is turning upside down.

President Trump took on the progressives like Snowden took on government, knowing full well that it will be at their own peril. The progressive democratic party, intent on destroying Trump, has taken our political system to new lows. Under progressive ideology, no longer does the will of the people carry until the next election cycle. Instead of abiding by the rules of Constitutional Law, the progressives prefer Saul Alinsky's "Rules for Radicals." Rule 5: "Ridicule is man's most potent weapon." There is no defense. It's irrational. It's infuriating. It also works as a key pressure point to force the enemy into concessions." Rule 8: "Keep the pressure on. Never let up." Keep trying new things to keep the opposition off balance. As the opposition masters one approach, hit them from the flank with something new."[42]

---

[42] *http://www.openculture.com/2017/02/13-rules-for-radicals.html*

As of this writing, there are 29 investigations related to Trump, which include 10 Federal Criminal Investigations, 8 State and Local Investigations and 11 Congressional Investigations, all designed to find reason for impeachment, which include 10 Federal Criminal Investigations, 8 State and Local Investigations and 11 Congressional Investigations, all designed to find reason for impeachment.[43] The Mueller Report became the progressive's best tool to keep Trump on the defense; Allinsky would be proud. The Mueller report failed to prove Russian collusion or interference in the 2016 Presidential election.[44] Meanwhile, the public endures actual mishandling of justice within the progressive movement, that has yet activated any investigations into Hillary's illegal email server, the phony Steele Dossier and FISA warrant, Comey, Strzok, Page, Clapper, Brennan, etc. Equal justice under the law requires equal treatment under existing laws. Trump is an enigma to the progressives in congress. Allinsky's rules work IF the target reacts as expected. No matter one's political stripe, Trump has demonstrated that our democratic form of government does not equate to a 'social democracy' and can continue to thrive despite progressive pressure.

My mission is not only to make some of our most recent political and physical occurrences understandable but also to offer real solutions that the average American can easily participate in. Keep in mind, that to have a constitution that guarantees limited centralized government in favor of individual states and personal rights that ensure our precious freedoms, comes with a hefty price; that price is participation in the system. Every citizen has the duty to participate in order to keep that freedom. Freedom cannot be taken from us unless we give it away.

History is an ever-evolving part of life with its facts and traditions passed from generation to generation, guaranteeing one thing that cannot be taught; wisdom. In similar fashion, those with the desire to alter reality can easily do so by altering the facts of history, or worse, omit them entirely. The progressive

[43] *https://www.nytimes.com/interactive/2019/05/13/us/politics/trump-investigations.html*
[44] *https://www.justice.gov/storage/report.pdf*

movement in this country is attempting to alter the facts of our history through Common Core education, allowing interpretation of historical facts to suit the needs of a progressive agenda. A strong centralized government with far reaching political and economic mandates can easily force publishers of school texts to print what is socially and politically acceptable to its agenda of transforming the American Constitution and the freedoms inherent in its Bill of Rights. Pre-World War II Germany attempted to alter history by ordering the burning of all historical books in favor of the tyrannical teaching of the emerging ideologically motivated racist and white supremacist doctrines of Nazism.[45]

It is, therefore, the responsibility of every American to never allow the contents of our Constitution to be altered in favor of political expediency or ideological utopia. In 1828, Arthur Stansbury wrote the *Elementary Catechism on the Constitution of the United States*.[46] During the first century of our country, great care was taken to ensure that our schools educate our children about the most enlightened system of government ever created. Stansbury's text consisted of 322 questions and answers on the Constitution and functioning of our federal government in a concise guide for use in public schools.

The following are specific questions and answers from *Elementary Catechism on the Constitution of the United States* were included in the text of Miracles and Massacres by Glenn Beck.[47] A few of the key questions and answers are reproduced here exactly as presented, to highlight the need for diligence in the upcoming battle of Common Core education and are pertinent to this current discussion and the administrative policies affecting education today. It is my experience as a former high school educator in the NYC school system in the 1970s and early 1980s that once a school board is monetarily or politically influenced by progressive ideology, history is lost.

---

[45] http://en.wikipedia.org/wiki/Nazi book burnings
[46] http://www.constitution.org/cmt/stansbury/elementary catechism on the constitution.pdf
[47] Beck, Glenn, and Kevin Balfe. Miracles and massacres: true and untold stories of the making of America. Threshold Editions, 2013.

Q 181: Who executes the laws which Congress have made, that is, who takes care that everybody shall obey the laws?
A: The President of the United States

Q 182: Can he make the law?
A: Not at all. These two powers, of *making* law, and *executing* law, are kept by the Constitution, entirely separate; the power that makes the law cannot execute it, and the power that executes the law cannot make it. (One of these powers is called the Legislative, and the other is called the Executive power.)

Q 266: Why are not Judges elected from time to time, like Members of the House of Representatives and Senators? And why may they not be removed from their offices unless they are proved to be guilty of great offences?
A: If Judges held their places at the mere good pleasure of the people, they would be greatly tempted to act in a partial and improper manner in order to please those who chose them to office, and to keep their favor; but when they know that no man or number of men can turn them out of office so long as they do their duty, they administer justice without fear and with an equal regard to all who ask it.

Q 267: Why then should not Legislators hold their office in the same way?
A: Because they make the laws, while Judges only explain and apply them. It would be very dangerous to liberty to give our law makers power for life; they require restraint lest they should become our tyrants; therefore their time of office is made short, so that if he people thought them unwise or unfaithful they may refuse to give them the office again.

Q 296: The majority of the people of any State may certainly alter its laws, provided they do not violate the Constitution: but may the Constitution itself be altered?

A: Yes. The constitution being nothing more than an expression of the will of the people of the United States, is at all times within their own power, and they may change it as they like, but it ought not to be changed till it is very clearly shown to be the wish of the people.

Q 300: What security have we that the Constitution will be observed?
A: The President, Members of Congress, the Members of all the State Legislatures, and all public officers of the United States, and of each one of the States, takes an oath, when they enter upon their several offices, to obey the Constitution. But the great security for its observance lies in the wisdom and excellence of the Constitution itself, and the conviction of the whole people of the United States, that it is for their true interest to observe it inviolate. It has been tried for fifty years, and has done more to render this nation peaceable, powerful and happy than any form of government that ever existed among men.

Q 308: What do you understand by these expressions?
A: In a free country like ours, every citizen has a right to express his opinion of the character and conduct of our rulers, and of the laws they make for our government; to forbid this, or punish it, would be highly dangerous to our liberty. If those chosen by their fellow citizens to rule the State, rule in a foolish or wicked manner, it ought to be known, that they may be speedily turned out of office, but if nobody might find fault with them without danger of punishment, their bad conduct would never be exposed, and they might continue in power to the great injury of us all. The right to speak our opinions is the freedom of speech; and the right to print them, that they may be read by others, is the freedom of the press.

It would be wise to understand and make public our founding principles; failure to do so is an open invitation for the progressive takeover of this country. Take heed that it is no accident that our country, the innovator of a free press, now ranks 46th in *freedom* of the press. I fear it is public ignorance and not stupidity that is driving the forces of the progressive movement. Words have meaning—allowing euphemistic phrases to replace standard Constitutional language affecting the future of this country is unacceptable and can only be stopped by an informed citizenry.

Let's Talk Indifference

History is an ever-evolving part of life with its facts and traditions passed from generation to generation, guaranteeing that one thing cannot be taught: wisdom. In similar fashion, those with the desire to alter reality can easily do so by altering the facts of history, or worse, omit them entirely. Recent events in Charlottesville, VA, typify the movement of 'progressive' socialists in this country to cleanse history of any memory of slavery. The movement is spreading to cities across America, but the simple removal of confederate statues will not cleanse the history of slavery nor is its intent. The target is the constitution, not slavery. Have you noticed that our country seems to be going crazy? Every historical American tradition is under scrutiny. The appearance of new terms like the Alt-right and groups of violent people suddenly showing up at peaceful rallies to instigate violence, on cue when the media cameras begin to roll, is no accident. Doesn't it seem odd that any attempt to bring stability is labeled as racist? To the astute historian, none of this is new. Countries and nations lose control when their citizens become indifferent, confused, or worse, unaware of what is occurring.

Today, 'western' people who willingly capitulate to extremist group of all stripes, in the name of tolerance, multiculturalism, political correctness, or just plain stupidity, only embolden those hell-bent on the destruction of this country. It has been said that history tends to repeat itself, but few ever seek to know why. Present day America is experiencing the ugly side of democracy—indifference. The United States is unlike any country ever formed. It is not a copy of other countries and is the only country where the PEOPLE were given the power and right to run the country. Our constitution destroys monarchies and dictatorships. It was written as a lasting document, changed only by constitutional conventions, not public opinion.

The enemies of our Constitution know that those who benefit from its existence can destroy it, if given the right incentives. Democracies depend on staying ever vigilant to Constitutional law. Democracies are destroyed by indifference and accepting radical thinking that play on emotions rather than intellect. Radicals never address the 'real' issues, but instead attack individuals. President Trump is a prime target for activism because he has no ties to the political elite. Enabled by Federal Communications Commission (FCC) mergers, TV media has become the visual arm of the activists because they are controlled and financed by six major corporations: GE, Newscorp, Disney, Viacom, Time Warner, and CBS. In 1983, there were 50 diverse companies contributing balanced news to the American people.[48] It should be noted that most owners of these mega media corporations have discrete ties to the liberal agenda and want nothing less than control over all advertising and 'how' people think. Did you know that the presidents of CBS and ABC have brothers that were top officials in the Obama administration? Is it any wonder that President Obama received none of the harsh treatment or bad press President Trump is receiving?

Keep in mind the progressive movement was formulated in part by the ultra-liberal writings of Saul Alinsky, the father of community activism and mentor to Barack Obama. Alinsky's most notable contribution to activism was his 12 Rules for Radicals, the last of which (Rule 12) is a blueprint for todays media:

---

[48] *http://www.businessinsider.com/these-6-corporations-control-90-of-the-media-in-america-2012-6*

"Pick the target, freeze it, personalize it, and polarize it. Cut off the support network and isolate the target from sympathy. Go after people and not institutions; people hurt faster than institutions."[49]

The destruction of confederate statues, monuments, and long-held historical traditions, stirs hatred against the individuals who represent slavery (Rule 12). What people don't know is that this is community organizing at its best. New terms have emerged like the 'Alt-right', a description of race-infused extreme conservativism that believes in white supremacy, violence, and the belief that white people are superior to the black race, and should therefore dominate society. The term Alt-right is used in the media to focus on the people (Rule 12) as a means of changing principles. These statues represent our history and once lost, future generations will have no reference or 'wisdom' gained from our past. The intent is to convince people that the U.S. was founded on flawed and unjust principles and therefore MUST be destroyed. By linking 'slavery' to the very names that formed our country, the progressives can link whatever followed in U.S. ideology as also being flawed and in need of change. Remember Obama's campaign slogans; "to fundamentally change America" and "hope and change"? What was never asked was . . . what exactly are we changing?

Obama's roots in community organizations in Chicago was under the mentorship of Saul Alinsky; is there any question now as to what that change was to be? America is silently being taken apart in the name of making it better, without ever describing what 'better' means. Our children see only what the media presents—biased reporting. Modern parents are not teaching their children our traditions. Information overload, confusion, and indifference are the tools of the progressive movement. Like all socialist countries, any questioning of prevailing thought is met with swift condemnation, isolation, and eventual incarceration for speaking your mind. How's that free speech working out for you?

[49] http://www.fbcoverup.com/docs/library/2016-08-27-Saul-Alinsky-12-Rules-for-Radicals-Obama-Hillary-Playbook-posted-Aug-27-2016.pdf

Laws are being pushed through state legislators to criminalize counter thinking. In 2016, the Washington Times reported that the California legislature presented a landmark bill that would make it illegal to engage in climate-change dissent.[50]

So what's next in the progressive playbook? Once the statues are gone, the issue of slavery will focus on higher goals. How long will it take for those who seek to destroy our country to focus their attention on our founding fathers? When George Washington was 11 years old, he inherited 10 slaves; by the time of his death, 317 slaves lived at Mount Vernon, including 123 owned by Washington.[51] Thomas Jefferson, the father of the Abolitionist movement, worked to gradually end the practice of slavery while himself owned hundreds of African slaves throughout his adult life.[52] Do you have any idea how many monuments, buildings, and cities, let alone currency, bear the names of Washington and Jefferson? **Watch out *Washington Times*** This is 'low hanging fruit' for the activists. The State of New York was one of the original 13 colonies that formed the United States. New York was named after the 17th century Duke of York, who himself was a slave owner.[53] *(Note: I am a former New Yorker; what will I then call myself?)* Slavery, in the hands of the activists, is an emotional tool used to whip up anxiety, hatred, and the 'get even' attitude so necessary for a revolution.

No one can predict the future, but as a student of history, I can attest that every country that collapsed under the relentless pressure of activism, large centralized governments, the promise of utopia or tyrants disguised as benevolent servants to the people, all had their middle class destroyed. Most notably, the entitlement programs ended, leaving the economy in shambles and dependent on government for mere survival. Our country may not be perfect and surely there are parts of our history that are ugly by today's standards, but

[50] *http://www.washingtontimes.com/news/2016/jun/2/calif-bill-prosecutes-climate-change-skeptics/*
[51] *https://www.google.com/search?q=how+many+slaves+did+George+Washing+have&oq=how+many+slaves+did+-George+Washing+have&aqs=chrome..69i57.14175j0j8&sourceid=chrome&ie=UTF-8*
[52] *https://en.wikipedia.org/wiki/Thomas_Jefferson_and_slavery*
[53] *https://en.wikipedia.org/wiki/New_York_(state)*

'we the people' must decide between true freedom and false promises. History is there as a lesson for all to learn. Information overload is leading this country into chaos. Indifference will close the deal.

CHAPTER THREE

GOVERNMENT DECEPTION AND THE 4ᵀᴴ BRANCH OF THE FEDERAL GOVERNMENT

Government Deception

Toward the end of Obama's presidency, it appeared that political deception was on the rise. The U.S. population was just beginning to get a glimpse as to the realities of a progressive government. Words have meaning and the interpretations of words change over time, either by intention or by cultural conditions; the key is knowing when deception is occurring. It must be clearly understood that "Liberalism" and "Progressivism" as an economic mindset, are not synonymous. "Liberalism" focuses on using taxpayer money to help better society. Progressivism focuses on using government power to make large institutions play by a "set of rules." A "progressive government" therefore, exists for the purpose of redefining the fulfillment of human capacities as the primary task of the state.[54]

The Progressive Movement began in America in the 20th century, in cities where settlement workers and reformers, who were interested in helping those facing harsh conditions at home and at work, needed protection from oppression. Progressivism was embraced by American presidents like Theodore Roosevelt, Woodrow Wilson, Franklin Roosevelt, Lyndon Johnson and others. As the industrial revolution transformed migrant workers into

---

[54] *http://www.huffingtonpost.com/david-sirota/whats-the-difference-betw_b_9140.html*

corporate employees, the progressive movement moved from helping the oppressed to initiating social oppression. In general, the progressive philosophy is synonymous with advocating gradual social, political, and economic reform—moving society away from democratic principles.

Historically, no democracy has survived more than two hundred years. The reasons are many but there is one cause worth remembering. Democracy requires continued diligence and responsibility to founding principles. With each generation, responsibility wanes in favor of political or social groups acting on their own behalf. The result is that eventually all responsibilities (dictated by founding principles) are deferred to others who are willing to take responsibility.[55] Sooner or later those political or social groups get infiltrated by the default government. This is *Socialism*, euphemistically renamed *Progressivism*. In this manner the U.S. population never experiences social change until once again, the government becomes oppressive. By that time, it's usually too late to recover.

The classic modern example is a group called *Democracy for America*. This sounds like a group to get behind for sure. Keep in mind, words have meaning! Democracy for America has been redefined by the Democratic Party as a "progressive political action committee," the result of which became the basis for the then candidate Barack Obama's platform slogan... "Change We Can Believe In."[56] What Americans actually voted for and approved, was to fundamentally move America from a Democracy toward Socialism, under the guise of Progressivism.

It is at this point one must ask the question: did most Americans who voted for Obama actually understand that Progressivism is not a better form of Democracy? Did they really understand that the word "progress" in Progressivism doesn't mean a better way to enhance Democracy but instead, is an ideology that moves a population more toward Socialism? There are only two

---

[55] *http://thefreeandthebrave.blogspot.com/2009/10/can-democracy-last-longer-than-200.html*
[56] *http://en.wikipedia.org/wiki/List_of_U.S._presidential_campaign_slogans#2008*

possibilities: perhaps they did understand, in which case our country is in for a rude awakening or they have been duped into an emotional, "adolescent" desire to rid the country of what they might believe were constitutional restrictions on their lives. Either possibility ends up in the same place; America loses its' identity.

For purposes of this discussion, consider the following example: Obamacare was sold to the public as a progressive effort to convince all citizens that had a "right" to healthcare; no such "right" exists. Younger Americans embraced the concept but never read the fine print. After all the perceived benefits, including the Obama rhetoric of keeping you own doctor, keeping your present healthcare plan and saving up to $2,500 per year, was the statement that "ALL CITIZENS MUST JOIN THE HEALTHCARE EXCHANGE."

The progressive method of "over promising and under delivering" became evident when Americans in general, realized that none of Obama's promises about "The Healthcare Affordability Act" (Obamacare) were true and they really had no choice whether to participate or not. Those who failed to join the "exchange" would be penalized the cost of the exchange policy on their tax return. The IRS became the enforcement arm for Obamacare. The Trump administration's promise of "repeal or replace" Obamacare faced the progressive "talking points" of "how can the Republicans even consider rescinding the 20 million Americans now covered by Obamacare?" The reality that the 20 million Americans were forced to join the "exchange," is of little consequence. Deception is a wonderful tool in controlling a population.

Months into Obama's second term, the lies and hidden agendas within Progressivism began to emerge, including scandals of enormous significance to the economic security of this country; i.e., expanded government control (regulation), de-privatization of our healthcare system (1/5th of our gross national product), open borders, lax immigration policies, sanctuary cities for undocumented immigrants, NAFTA and the Iranian Nuclear Deal, just to name a few.

The North American Free Trade Agreement (NAFTA), for example, is a progressive movement attempting to redistribute the wealth in America between Canada and Mexico. Just the tone of what was just stated, has probably "tuned out" many of you reading this. But bear with me by considering the following realities of NAFTA:

John is an American worker, who earns $22.50/hour making chrome plated widgets for a major corporation that has 5,500 employees, also making the same widgets. John has great healthcare benefits, a partially paid retirement plan with a company matched 401K plan, owns a house in the suburbs of New York, has two cars, and is married with 2.5 children. The board of directors and CEO of John's company were looking into ways of boosting their profits. The company tried to reduce company benefits and freeze salaries but the company's union, who fought hard for these benefits (now seen as entitlements) threatened to strike.

The CEO, being aware of NAFTA, decided it was time to investigate the possibility of farming out the production of their widgets to Mexico, where they found a company who manufacturers' the identical chrome plated widgets for far less money than in the U.S. John's company struck a deal with the Mexican company, bypassing American government regulations due to NAFTA. Soon John's company had doubled their profit margins by making their widgets in Mexico and shipping them back to the U.S. without tariffs (taxes on imports), thanks to NAFTA.

One day John's company sent a "dear John letter" (no pun intended) to half of its employees informing them that they were laid off. John fortunately was not one of them, at least for now.

The laid off workers immediately applied for State and Company funded unemployment benefits, as approved by the U.S. Secretary of Labor.[57] Six months later John's company decided to merge their company with their Mexican counterparts, in Mexico and close their plant in New York. After 18 years of service, John was unemployed, along with thousands of other employees from different such companies around the country because of NAFTA guidelines. John and his family's lifestyle were in shambles, dependent on an ever-growing demand for government subsidies (entitlements).

Although the story is fictitious, it demonstrates the actual result of NAFTA on the American worker and our economy. The salient message hidden within NAFTA, which caused President Trump to openly condemn NAFTA as a "disaster for the American economy, is that without "tariffs" on goods and services produced outside the U.S., American workers are doomed.

Keep in mind that tariffs on products are paid for by the consumer not by the country of origin. In 2019, President Trump actually used the power of the tariff on Mexican goods, not to balance fair trade with Mexico, as with the fictitious NAFTA example above, but to force Mexico to enact their immigration laws to stop the flow of illegal immigrant 'caravans' from using Mexico as a free passage route to the U.S./Mexican border. The Progressives in congress realized that their desire for open borders was doomed if Trump succeeded in doing an 'end around' congress via tariffs and attempted to whip the American people into a frenzy over increased prices because of the tariffs. Fortunately, the economic consequences of tariffs on Mexican goods was enough for Mexico to sign a deal with the U.S. to stop the caravans before the tariff deadline.

So, who wins by having "free trade?" The answer, once again, lies within the Progressive mindset of "over promising and under delivering." Mega corporations (who represent the rich), enjoying

[57] http://www.csmonitor.com/USA/Politics/2011/0209/Unemployment-101-Who-pays-for-jobless-benefits-anyway

the benefits from NAFTA, hire lobbyists and donate heavily to political parties and candidates to win political favor. This is not the forum Progressivism 101 but understand when Capitalism is replaced by Progressivism, society changes dramatically. Progressivism requires a greater, more powerful central government intrusion. Capitalism enhances the wealth of the middle class, while Progressivism tends to eliminate the middle class, increasing government entitlement programs (ask John), and reducing our country's standard of living.

Progressives want the population to demonize the rich as the reason why "the people" are poor; however, the Progressives **are the rich** and once in control will have the power to perpetuate the myth while reaping the benefits. Posing popular "emotional" questions like: "what's wrong with making the rich pay their fair share?" or "what's wrong with redistributing the wealth of our nation among the poor?" is the progressives way dividing the nation.

With no disrespect intended toward any particular group, consider the following facts before buying the myth:

- The rich supply most of the jobs. If progressivism replaces capitalism, the middle class entrepreneur disappears. If the rich move their companies out of the country for higher profits (NAFTA), who will you work for? The government will become your de facto employer.

- In 1964 (Johnson administration), our country declared a war on poverty.[58] Some 50 years later and trillions of dollars poured into the effort, 15% of the U.S. population is still in poverty—slightly more than it was in 1964.

- NAFTA has cost the U.S. economy 700,000 jobs and huge trade deficits.

In fact, pick any government funded program designed as; a "war on drugs, crime, cancer or education equality" and see

---

[58] *http://budget.house.gov/waronpoverty*

how successful it was. Government funded programs spend taxpayer money with little or no accountability. The justification is always at least we tried![59]

Free trade has been the signature agenda platform of giant corporations, political donors and the progressive agenda. For a sitting president to openly rebuke Free Trade agreements, is political suicide. President Trump is the first president to actually explain to the people why economically, NAFTA and other World Trade Organization agreements are potential disasters for the American economy. President Trump is first and foremost a consummate businessman, who understands the U.S. cannot remain solvent with ever increasing trade deficits. He also understands that if the U.S. government wants to dabble in business, it must show a profit. What company in the history of the world can remain solvent without a strong profit and loss statement? There is no accountability with socialism because the money you receive and spend is not your own and as Margaret Thatcher once said. "The trouble with Socialism is that eventually you run out of other people's money."[60]

One of the most profitable and successful private business corporations in America is Walmart. Few of us can remember that Walmart began in 1962, embracing its "Made in America" pledge that all product is produced, manufactured and assembled in America. Walmart, (like the example of John's fictitious widget company) found that its' board of directors and CEO could buy and sell products for less, while increasing their profits, if they partnered with Mexico, China and other countries. I dare say that a quick look on any Walmart shelf will find Made in China or Made in Mexico labels on most products. The Federal Trade Commission recently forced Walmart to scrub its "Made in America" slogan from its website; another example why NAFTA is bad for America.[61]

[59] http://www.huffingtonpost.com/jeff-faux/nafta-twenty-years-after_b_4528140.html
[60] https://www.snopes.com/fact-check/other-peoples-money
[61] https://www.forbes.com/sites/lauraheller/2016/06/28/walmart-made-in-the-usa-products-fact-or-fiction/#23b5ecc23a2b

Free Market vs Capitalism

To truly understand economics, one must understand that wealth, goods and services, profits and job creation, depend largely on "supply and demand," using a universally accepted rate of exchange.

For the purpose of this discussion, I will only address government involvement in economics and not the sovereign rights of individuals to do business apart from government regulation.

The realities of economic "free trade" go well beyond textbook definitions due to social and cultural factors.

A *capitalist* system and a *free market* system are economic environments where dictates of supply and demand are the main factors determining price and production of goods and services. Although the two economic systems are based on the law of supply and demand, these systems are different.

- **Capitalism** is an economic system based on ownership of the factors of production. Some key features of capitalism are competition between companies and owners, private ownership and motivation to generate a profit. The production and pricing of goods and services is determined by the free market, or supply and demand.

- A **Free Market** system is based solely on supply and demand in world markets, without intervention from outside government forces, tariffs or regulations. In a free market system, a buyer and a seller transact freely, only when they voluntarily agree on the price of a good or a service.[62]

Capitalism is focused on the **creation** of *wealth* and *ownership* of capital as well as factors of production, whereas a *Free Market* system is focused on the **exchange** of wealth, or goods and services. Due to the ever-growing presence of governmental

---

[62] http://www.investopedia.com/ask/answers/042215/what-difference-between-capitalist-system-and-free-market-system.asp

regulations, the *"Progressives"* have seized the opportunity of using greater government control (for the country's own good) as a cover to move the country toward Socialism.

Government Overreach

One clearly has to understand that government mandates are euphemisms for *law*. The incremental abuse of constitutional power, seemingly approved by Congress, empowers the federal government. It is my opinion that our government was rapidly approaching a point in its progressive agenda that has minimal need for congressional oversight, as witnessed by the numerous scandals against our Constitution and public at large. The Constitution provides specific enumerated powers to be exercised by the Federal Government. The main functions of the Federal Government are to create and enforce laws to ensure order and stability within society, to coin money and regulate its value, ensuring a stable economy and to raise and maintain our armed forces for our national defense. The Executive branch of government also has a specific degree of constitutional interpretation by the "executive order" in times of national emergencies that must have a constitutional basis.

Most citizens are not familiar with the specifics of the Constitution and are dependent on their elected congressional representatives to ensure their interests are being well protected. To an unsuspecting public, rouge government officials or policies can easily be implemented. The Constitution was designed to limit the ability of the federal government to act autonomously but cannot stop it from occurring. Continuous scandalous events within our government have made it difficult for the public to evaluate. Public diligence is the only defense against policies not in the best interest of the country.

Examples of Government Overreach

Common Core

The Obama administration increased national control over our schools via the *Common Core Curriculum Initiative*. Common Core is a new curriculum developed by a panel of so-called education (government) experts. The administration tried to turn Common Core into a national curriculum by offering states increased federal educational funding if they imposed Common Core's curriculum on their public schools. In short, the government was using taxpayer money to fundamentally alter what students will learn about this country. This is yet another example of the government using tax money from the people to bribe states into obeying federal mandates.

Education is the responsibility of individual states. The Federal government, under the Obama administration, really did not put the common core curriculum together, instead it was the National Governors Association that discussed the creation of Common Core state standards in 2007, a year before Obama's first term.[63] Obama incorporated Common Core principles into his "Race to the Top" educational initiative,[64] by developing a 4 billion dollar grant program to provide incentives for states to implement Common Core. Federal funding rather than debate became the driving force.

Common Core curriculum fit perfectly into Obama's progressive ideology of "Hope and Change." For Obama it was all about controlling the progressive narrative for his upcoming presidential election. One must recognize the pattern of the progressive agenda; it's all about urgency, no time to waste, our country's future is at stake. By using emotional hooks rather than constitutional debate, "agenda's" get implemented. Remember that Obamacare was passed without congressional debate. One fifth of the American economy got redirected to a "new" healthcare

---

[63] *http://www.politifact.com/wisconsin/statements/2013/oct/24/sondy-pope/how-much-federal-government-involved-common-core-s*
[64] *https://en.wikipedia.org/wiki/Race_to_the_Top*

system that no one even read. Nancy Pelosi put it best to congress; *"we have to pass the bill so that you can find out what's in it."*[65] Hardly a democratic process, unless agenda driven. Once compromises are made for political reasons and not for educational reasons, the intent becomes murky.

Critics of the Common Core say it dumbs down education by replacing traditional English literature and history with informational texts; replacing actual facts with designer history.[66] Traditionally, education is a "state" controlled responsibility. Having a centralized federal educational platform is tantamount to educational suicide and with it goes diversity of opinions, such as *Freedom of Speech*, which is a clever way to circumvent the first amendment of our Constitution. As an aside, the Common Core curriculum also separates the parent from educating their child as well. Think it can't happen? Historically, this is exactly what the Nazis did with the youth of Germany... indoctrinate and separate.[67]

It's not enough that the Federal Government has granted itself legislative and implied powers never designated by the constitution; the Federal Government is now expanding its "ownership" conquests into private enterprise. Along with the "corporate" auto, banking, mortgages, airlines and other industries, the government has set its sights on federal monies to colleges.

On a bus tour through New York and Pennsylvania, that began August 22, 2013, Obama gave a series of poll-boosting speeches to University campuses, as part of his "Foundation for the Middle Class" to reform higher education's increased tuition costs.[68] President Obama used the Federal Government's increased control over student loans to push for greater federal control over college administration, graduation rates and tuition costs.[69] Obama told these young minds that he "saved" GM from bankruptcy (implying he can do the same

[65] *https://www.youtube.com/watch?v=hV-05TLiiLU*
[66] *http://www.infowars.com/common-core-nationalizes-and-dumbs-down-public-school-curriculum*
[67] *http://victorygirlsblog.com/common-core-and-the-hitler-youth-can-it-happen-here*
[68] *http://www.buffalonews.com/city-region/erie-county/obama-trip-to-buffalo-emphasizes-ambitious-plan-to-control-college-costs-20130822*
[69] *http://dailycaller.com/2013/08/22/obama-pushes-for-more-federal-control-over-education*

for higher education), while neglecting to tell students that the government essentially owned GM should GM fail to meet their reorganization obligations.

The government has no authority or mechanism to own a private industry. Obama did not save the auto industry, as he would have the inexperienced college mind believe, he used *"Quantitative Easing"* funds to save the union in return for their loyalty and ownership. Government assistance in higher education comes from taxpayer money and as such allows government a degree of control over the industry of higher education.

The real purpose of this meaningless bus tour was to rally the upcoming, young workforce into accepting government assistance as part of their financial portfolio. These young minds do not have life experience and are easily taught to embrace financial support from wherever it is presented. These young minds and pocketbooks were also necessary to initially prop up Obama's Healthcare Affordability Act. As a point of entry into the private sector, the government has attempted to "rig" the outcome to ensure that it's only a matter of time before complete government compliance is the norm.

IRS

This is not the forum for a full IRS discussion or disclosure, but certain facts need to be known before one can understand the significance of the IRS scandals. Suffice to say, the IRS has been given undue powers based not on constitutional law but federal government edicts. The IRS was technically set up by President Lincoln to fund the costs of the Civil War in the Act of 1862, which established the office of commissioner of the IRS. All that did was create the office of the commissioner, who is just a figure head of a private corporation, just as the commissioner of the Federal Reserve is the head of the private corporation but has no legal or constitutional connection to the U.S. Government.

Not only is the collection of taxes a questionable function of the IRS but it is further scandalized by giving the IRS power to administer the financial implementation of the Affordable Care Act (Obama care) of 2010, where there is no legal precedent whatsoever. To implement this new responsibility, the IRS is merely a private corporation hired by the U.S. government as a collection agency. The IRS has been given illegal and unconstitutional "police" power to bypass almost any constitutional amendment without congressional approval and answers only to the Department of the Treasury, which is under the control of the Executive Branch of our government. *Translation: The IRS answers to the president and not congress.* Hence the ease and secrecy the IRS had to perpetrate its Gestapo-like tactics as well as the freedom to spend taxpayer money, (some 50+ million dollars) on lavish hotels, baseball games, entertainment, inappropriate (IRS) parties, etc.; none of which could occur under the watch of a diligent and responsible president or congress.[70]

If a government agency has autonomy, it can act independently of any of the conflicts of interest or moralities faced by the rest of the population. Jaimie Dupree, a Washington D.C. insider watchdog reported that "A new report shows the Internal Revenue Service routinely gave bonuses and time off awards to tax agency workers who had been disciplined internally for job-related misconduct, which included fraud, misuse of government credit cards and the failure to properly pay their federal taxes to Uncle Sam."[71] In short, the Treasury Inspector General found that 1,146 performance awards, some averaging over $1,000 of tax payer money, were issued to IRS workers despite misconduct that would have resulted in firing or jail time for non-government employees.

This scandal is a national eye-opener. More recently, the IRS was given the unconstitutional power to monitor "healthcare" decisions under Obamacare. An additional 16,000 IRS agents have been put on the government payroll to insure all citizens comply with the purchasing of healthcare coverage or face penalties inclusive

---

[70] http://politicalticker.blogs.cnn.com/2013/06/04/breaking-report-shows-lavish-spending-at-irs-conference
[71] http://www.wsbradio.com/weblogs/jamie-dupree/2014/apr/22/irs-gives-bonuses-workers-cited-misconduct

of garnishing tax returns, while providing "cover" for the illegal distribution of all medical and personal records to any government or law enforcement agency, on demand and without a warrant.

The IRS is a "corporation" which administers to the collection of taxes within the U.S.; however, the Constitution of the U.S. does not empower Congress to delegate any function to the IRS, nor does it have any jurisdiction in the 50 states. The Sixteenth Amendment of 1913, supposedly giving Congress the power to collect income taxes, was never ratified. Compelling evidence and documentation can be found in the book "The Law That Never Was."[72] The definition of "income tax" as written but not ever ratified is not a tax on wages or salaries but on the profit made from the investment of wages and salaries. Direct governmental lying and unfounded implications to the contrary, has placed FEAR into the minds of people. Regardless of the circumstances, the IRS has been "bestowed" powers making it the most brutal collection agency in the nation, answerable to only the president.

The IRS was caught targeting organizations, specifically conservative organizations who apply for 501(c) (4) status. This targeting was based on political leanings. The IRS decided, by filtering organizations that used the words "tea party" or "patriot," (NSA spying) they could slow down or stop altogether any opposition to the progressive movement (remember who is their boss). By not approving the same non-profit status for other political organizations, the IRS begins its reign of tyranny.

The White House claimed that they had no knowledge of this practice; the federal government lied. The acting IRS Commissioner, Steven Miller (the CEO of the "private" IRS Corporation) took the heat but was able to disclose to congress that he was not in charge during the time the IRS was given the green light to blatantly discriminate; instead we find that senior White House officials knew of the IRS activity all along.[73] The IRS official that oversaw the division that targeted conservative

---

[72] *http://www.mind-trek.com/practicl/tl16a.htm*

50

nonprofit groups was Lois Lerner.

At the House Oversight and Government Reform Committee hearings, charged with investigating the unethical and possible criminal activity of the IRS, Lerner took the 5th Amendment, protecting her (and the IRS) against possible self-incrimination.[74] It appears politics once again trumps (no pun intended) truth.

Keeping in mind the arm's length relationship the IRS has with the government, it is easy to understand why the Obama administration stated it had nothing to do with the IRS targeting conservative groups. Simply put, the IRS was hired by the US government, but is not part of or directly responsible, to the constitutional government of the U.S. The scam has perpetuated for over a century with its secret well maintained to keep the population unaware of the truth and in constant fear of IRS reprisals. Any attempt to expose the openly available truth about the IRS is shut down with military type efficiency, bypassing traditional due process. U.S. Government history textbooks have expunged any reference to the fraud that is the IRS.

The Department of Justice

The Department of Justice, during the Obama administration, was found to have seized the work and personal phone line messages of Associated Press (AP) reporters. This DOJ investigation came about because of an AP article on a foiled CIA terror plot where the AP disclosed specifics of the operation. These phone records were seized as part of an ongoing investigation into the AP's practices and which government officials they had used and have been using as sources.[75]

Then Attorney General Eric Holder claimed he didn't know the specifics because he had recused himself from the investigation. In a letter of protest sent to Eric Holder, AP President and CEO said: "There can be no possible justification for such an

[73] http://www.huffingtonpost.com/tag/steven-miller-irs-scandal
[74] http://www.cbsnews.com/news/lois-lerner-pleads-the-fifth-again-doesnt-testify-on-irs-targeting
[75] http://www.huffingtonpost.com/2013/05/13/ap-phone-records-doj-leaks_n_3268932.html

overbroad collection of the telephone communications of The Associated Press and its reporters. These records potentially reveal communications with confidential sources across all of the newsgathering activities undertaken by the AP during a two-month period, providing a road map to AP's newsgathering operations and disclosing information about AP's activities and operations that the government has no conceivable right to know."[76] He demanded the return of the phone records and destruction of all copies.

The scandal resides in the fact that the federal government literally bypassed constitutional rights of the free press because it was annoyed that government employees perhaps provided the leaks to the AP. It did so by strong-arming the AP to release all phone and sensitive privileged records to DOJ agents.[77] No one is above the law and allowing such untethered access without court order amounts again to tyranny.

It appears that the DOJ could care less about the constitutional protocols they were sworn to abide. In 2018 the DOJ, in conjunction with then-FBI Director James Comey, colluded in securing the now infamous, unverified Christopher Steele dossier to secure a FISA (Foreign Intelligence Surveillance Act) warrant to spy on Trump campaign advisor Carter Page. The FBI withheld vital information from the FISA court, the American public and Congress, until months later, that Steele had been paid to find his dirt on Trump by a firm doing political opposition research for the Democratic Party and for Democratic presidential candidate Hillary Clinton.[78]

Is it any wonder that government intelligence agencies can and often will participate illegal activities like seizing secret intelligence, not reporting the truth or prying into the private files of future administration officials? Spying and espionage are common techniques used by all intelligence agencies or political party but outright lying and cover-ups for political reasons is tyranny.

---

[76] *http://www.ap.org/Images/Letter-to-Eric-Holder_tcm28-12896.pdf*
[77] *http://www.washingtonpost.com/politics/justice-department-irs-scandals-challenge-obamas-civil-liberties-credibility/2013/05/14/d1bc-56bc-bcc7-11e2-9b09-1638acc3942e_story.html*
[78] *https://thehill.com/hilltv/rising/419901-fbi-email-chain-may-provide-most-damning-evidence-of-fisa-abuses-yet*

Secrecy is the key to its success but for every spy, there is a counter spy. In 1961 *Mad Magazine* launched a parody about the intelligence gathering community with a comic strip called "Spy vs. Spy." It featured two "bird like" agents involved in espionage activities, one is dressed in white, and the other in black, with identical features. The pair are constantly at war with each other, using a variety of booby-traps to inflict harm on the other. The spies usually alternate between victory and defeat. The strip was created to depict the activities of the Cold War, but the realities are, comic strip or otherwise, the storyline of illegal spying, wiretapping and the seizing of public records for intelligence gathering, goes on within all intelligence agencies and governments. The public only becomes aware when they get caught.[79]

James Rosen of Fox News

"The Federal Government Seizing E-mails & Telephone Records of Private Citizens."

James Rosen is a journalist and former television correspondent in Washington, D.C. for Fox News. On May 17, 2013, the *Washington Post* reported the United States Department of Justice had monitored Rosen's activities by tracking his visits to the State Department, through phone traces, timing of calls and his personal emails. This case is a quintessential scandal of First Amendment rights. As a journalist, Rosen was working on a story about North Korea. In an article appearing in the *New Yorker* it states: *"The search warrant for Rosen's e-mail account is the most troubling aspect of the scandal because in the search warrant application, prosecutors alleged that there was probable cause to believe that Rosen violated the Espionage Act of 1917."*[80]

Then, Attorney General Eric Holder, blatantly lied to Congress and overstepped his legal authority to go shopping for a Federal Judge willing to set aside a hundred years of constitutional privacy

[79] https://en.wikipedia.org/wiki/Spy_vs._Spy
[80] http://www.newyorker.com/online/blogs/newsdesk/2013/05/news-corp-vs-fox-news.html

rights of citizens. In short, the federal government decided to go into the private life of a news correspondent, naming him a criminal co-conspirator for simply doing his job as a journalist. What was at stake here is defending the right to operate as a member of the free press.

Since when is the Federal Government above the law? Since when can a federal official manipulate the Judiciary branch of government with impunity? Eric Holder not only lied to Congress (punishable by Perjury on a federal level carrying a possible sentence of five years in prison) claiming he knew nothing about the unconstitutional privacy invasion, but he was initially turned down by two federal judges but found a third to comply, perhaps by making a bogus case of a possible national security breach.

Recent statements by the National Security Administration (NSA) and the Department of Justice (DOJ), designed to quell public concern over privacy rights, were that "these agencies do not have the right, nor can ever get the right, to read personal emails or tap into cellphone communications." This begs the question, why collect all this communication data in the first place? The fact is the NSA, DOJ, CIA and FBI, as seen in the James Rosen case, can void privacy rights at will. Democratic Patrick Leahy, the chairman of the Senate Judiciary Committee at the time, authored a Senate bill to rewrite laws that lets "feds" read your e-mail without warrants.[81] Within days, public outcry for upholding first amendment rights forced Leahy to rescind his warrantless e-mail surveillance bill, demonstrating there is power in public opinion.[82]

The point is that our system of justice and constitutional law hangs in the balance. We must never forget how the Nazi party took over the stable German government, essentially establishing its precedent of untethered and illegal information gathering under the guise of national security, all of this spearheaded by the promises of a single man—Adolf Hitler.

---

[81] http://www.cnet.com/news/senate-bill-rewrite-lets-feds-read-your-e-mail-without-warrants
[82] http://www.cnet.com/news/leahy-scuttles-his-warrantless-e-mail-surveillance-bill

FBI Seizing Personal Records

Google, this nation's largest and most comprehensive information search engine, is also a gold mine for data collection. Under the guise of national security, the FBI petitioned a federal judge to order Google to release customer data records to the FBI without justification. In short, this is a blatant invasion of privacy. After an initial rejection, U.S. district Court Judge Susan Illston approved the order. The scandal lies in the reason why a Federal Judge would approve such an ill-advised action? Could it be that the Obama executive administration illegally used the FBI to do its dirty work of collecting personal data on every citizen in the U.S., under the guise of potential terrorism prevention? It would seem plausible since the same has occurred with the huge wireless phone company Verizon, where Federal authorities secured the personal data of every single user on its vast network.

As of this writing, further information has arisen showing that the National Security Agency (NSA) has been, for years, spying on every American by gaining access to not only phone records but also credit card accounts, health records[83], life insurance policies, Facebook contacts, Twitter accounts and just about any collectible data they want, without reason or warrant. The NSA's actions are part of the mandate of the Patriot Act to thwart terrorism. Amazing how phone numbers and credit card accounts help thwart terrorism but for years, having wide open borders, no immigration policy and no program to deport foreign felons is somehow OK. The scandal is an obliteration of the First Amendment as well as an overreach of executive authority.

The Patriot Act was an Act of the U.S. Congress that was signed into law by President George W. Bush on October 26, 2001, in response to the 9/11 terrorist attacks on American soil. The act was hastily put together and received near unanimous support by both houses of congress, giving great latitude to circumvent Constitutional restraints on invasion of privacy. After closer

[83] http://www.forbes.com/sites/scottgottlieb/2013/05/15/the-irs-raids-60-million-personal-medical-records

review, it was found that the "Act" gave the progressive movement the needed precedence to bridge Constitutional law. Some of the shortcomings of the Patriot Act are: giving authorization of indefinite detentions of immigrants, searches through which law enforcement officers search a home or business without the owner's or the occupant's permission or knowledge, the expanded use of National Security Letters, which allows the Federal Bureau of Investigation to search telephone, e-mail, and financial records without a court order; the expanded access of law enforcement agencies to business records, including library and financial records and the president's new ability to wiretap Americans' phone calls without a warrant, on the suspicion they might be a terrorist. This single piece of legislation raises the question of trading security for freedom and can be argued as the justification for the scandals mentioned in this section.

In Oct. 2015, the Inspector General of Homeland Security found and disciplined 41 secret service agents who illegally dug into the confidential personal files of Utah republican Jason Chaffetz, who chaired the House Committee on Oversight and Government Reform. Chaffetz had once applied for a job with the Secret Service years before he was elected to the House and agents were looking for something that might embarrass him, according to the Inspector General's report.[84] Does this act by government officials raise to the level of suspected terrorism or is it a bastardization of the Patriot Act for sinister purposes?

Benghazi Investigation

The events of September 11, 2012, in Benghazi, Libya, remain a mystery. The magnitude of the breach in international security, coupled with the non-disclosure of critical facts by responsible government officials to congressional review is unpredicted and makes difficult to assume there was no government liability. Statements that the White House, the Department of State and

---

[84] http://abcnews.go.com/Politics/41-secret-service-agents-disciplined-congressmans-personnel-file/story?id=39411746

former Secretary of State Hillary Clinton are all hiding something in the death of Ambassador Chris Stevens and three other U.S. Foreign Service officers are impossible to ignore. The White House released hundreds of emails related to Benghazi. The talking points delivered, after the attack, changed dramatically leaving the public to believe it was a random act whereas later revelations proved otherwise. Unprecedented are the outright and unpunished lies stated to the public.

E-mails, obtained by conservative watchdog group Judicial Watch, through a Freedom of Information Act request, include one in which then White House official Ben Rhodes edited the official narrative of the embassy attack as a spontaneous protest assault that never happened. The intent was to mislead the American people while protecting the president from damaging criticism so close to the 2010 elections.[85] The then U.S. Ambassador to the United Nations, Susan Rice, appeared on five TV news and commentary networks stating the entire event was due to a video. Facts later revealed that the video was a fabricated lie to hide the truth: a potential cover-up. The scandal resides in the cover-up and the extent government officials will go to keep it a secret. Although investigations were ongoing, the Obama administration further complicated the investigation by reappointing Susan Rice as his National Security Advisor. In doing so, Susan Rice was insulated from testimony in the Benghazi investigations by protection of Executive Power.

The fact remains that two ranking American Ambassadors and two Navy seals were sacrificed for reasons yet to be discovered. Condemning the actions (or lack thereof) that the Obama administration took, allegedly to hide the real agenda, leads any American citizen to seriously question the depths of possible deception the government is willing to take to uphold its agenda. Along with a complicit media, the tactic used to avoid public scrutiny and congressional action, demanded by their constituents, is to simply not speak of it any longer. Not until

[85] http://www.examiner.com/article/new-documents-reveal-benghazi-cover-up-emanated-from-white-house

the revealing email evidence was released did the media break its deafening silence.[86] There should be no question that our American constitutional government is about to disappear if the citizens don't take decisive action.

Gun Control

This scandal is an affront to the 2nd Amendment of the Constitution. The progressive agenda of past administrations has been the disarming the public. The attempts occur at almost every instance of a mass shooting. It is an opportunistic attitude to push an agenda, playing on people's emotions. Taking guns from law abiding citizens not only goes against our 2nd Amendment rights but also exposes the public to additional dangers in the eyes of a criminal mind. To date, administrations have met with stiff opposition, from the National Rifle Association and like organizations, yet that may change at any time. One clever way to circumvent the 2nd Amendment of the Constitution, that has been considered, is to assign gun control to an international body like the UN.[87] This consideration will limit U.S. access to weapons to protect against potential terrorist activity under the Patriot Act. History shows that an unarmed population can offer little resistance; the resulting historical realities of such action was the disarming of German citizens during the Nazi regime. Former Texas Attorney General Greg Abbott seized the moment stating that: "if U.S. Government signs a UN agreement on gun control, the State of Texas will sue the Federal government for treason."[88]

On September 13, 2013, President Obama addressed the 4,000 in attendance at the Washington Navy Yard memorial services for the 12 victims of the mass shooting by former navy reservist Aaron Alexis. He called for a "transformation" in the nation's gun laws to address an epidemic of gun violence. He said, "no other advanced nation endures the kind of gun violence seen in the United States" and blamed mass shootings in America on

---

[86] http://www.scribd.com/doc/110758358/Executive-Summary-Brief-Benghazi
[87] http://www.gunsandammo.com/2013/09/27/what-the-united-nations-arms-trade-treaty-means-to-you
[88] http://www.statesman.com/news/news/abbott-warns-arms-treaty-could-spur-texas-to-sue/nZ7K4

laws that fail "to keep guns out of the hands of criminals and dangerous people."[89]

Having a national audience to speak to doesn't give a president a license to distort the truth. Newsmax reported that "Europe Has the Same Rate of Multiple Victim Shootings as the United States."[90] In the December 16, 2012 article by Daniel Greenfield, he states: "The media typically spins these mass shootings as an American phenomenon. They suggest we ought to be more like Europe, with their strong gun control laws, because then we would not have these problems. If you look at a per capita rate, the rates of multiple-victim public shootings in Europe and the United States over the last 10 years have been fairly similar to each other."

After every mass shooting that has occurred during Obama's presidency, was the opportunity to push for stricter gun laws, as he did in the aftermath of the elementary school shooting in Newtown, Connecticut, that killed 20 first graders and six staff. The acts of violence in Newtown and the Washington D.C. Naval yard are tragic and may even point out laxity in basic security measures but it is beyond comprehension that a U.S. military naval base can be breached, leading to violent massacre because trained military personnel are unarmed. Closer scrutiny reveals that in every mass shooting, whether in the U.S. or in Europe, was perpetrated by individuals who have mental disorders, or are on psychotropic drugs or they are just plain criminals. Not a single shooting was committed by someone considered to be without mental aberrations. It is mind boggling to think that disarming law-abiding citizens will keep guns out of the hands of criminals or the deranged. What possible questions, given stricter gun control, would identify a criminal? Why would a criminal seek legal means to get a gun? A criminal is a person who does not regard the law. Will a law stop a criminal from choosing to break the law and acquire a firearm?

[89] http://www.cnn.com/2013/09/22/politics/obama-navy-yard
[90] http://www.frontpagemag.com/2012/dgreenfield/europe-has-same-rate-of-multiple-victim-shootings-as-the-united-states

The continual argument for stricter gun registration laws are for the only purpose of disarming the law-abiding citizen, under the ruse that it will somehow keep guns from the criminal. An armed citizenry can offer resistance to oppression, which is the very reason for the 2nd Amendment. The mentally unstable, and those hell-bent on violence or aggression, will seek out the weak and defenseless to achieve their ultimate goal. A total of 62 mass shooting murders have taken place since 1990, all of which against the unarmed or the defenseless.

The most glaring example for the need to uphold our 2nd Amendment rights took place on June 16, 2016 when Omar Mateen, swore allegiance to Abu Bakr al-Baghdadi before he opened fire at the Pulse Nightclub in Orlando Florida, killing 49 and wounding 53 others.[91]

After a three hour standoff, police finally took Mateen down but what if during the rampage a legally armed citizen, be it a patron or staff member, might have been in position to stop Mateen? This simple question is what sets the progressives "hair on fire." Their immediate progressive response would be that the armed citizen would be taking the law into his own hands. This would be a reasonable objection but in the defense of one' life, the law on "self-defense" is clear. ***Proportional Response:*** *"The use of self-defense must also match the level of the threat in question. In other words, a person can only employ as much force as required to remove the threat. If the threat involves deadly force, the person defending themselves can use deadly force to counteract the threat."*[92]

I would ask those that do not agree to ask themselves; if you were looking down the barrel of a rifle or gun pointed at your head, by a mad man, a terrorist or just a mentally disturbed citizen, with the intent to end your life, would you object to your 2nd Amendment right to defend yourself?

[91] https://en.wikipedia.org/wiki/2016_Orlando_nightclub_shooting
[92] http://criminal.findlaw.com/criminal-law-basics/self-defense-overview.html

In an ABC 20/20 segment with John Stossel, he interviews Tom Palmer, who sued and won a favorable decision in the Federal Appeals Court for Washington D.C. to reverse its ban on private ownership of firearms.[93] Since the firearm ban took effect, murder and violent crime with a weapon in Washington DC skyrocketed, as it has in every other state with similar firearm bans. The court had no choice but to rescind the ban, dealing a serious blow to the Progressive agenda. This is not the forum for psychological analysis but it can be safely said that even criminals seek to avoid situations where retaliation is a possibility. In short, the best deterrent against a criminal with a gun is a victim unwilling to concede.

The Department of Homeland Security

A more sinister side to the gun and ammunition story goes much deeper into the labyrinth of a progressive takeover of our culture and rights. In August 2013, the Associated Press and other watch dog news organizations reported that, the Department of Homeland Security may in fact become the enemy of the people. In the August 7, 2013 article by Anthony Gucciardi of Global Research, (an article that should have become front page news), he states: "the DHS has openly established extensive Constitution free zones in which your Fourth Amendment does not exist."[94] The Fourth Amendment to the United States Constitution is the part of the Bill of Rights that "prohibits unreasonable searches and seizures and requires any warrant to be judicially sanctioned and supported by probable cause."[95]

The Department of Homeland Security (DHS) and the Patriot Act were created in response to the September 11th attacks. The Department of Defense is responsible for military operations abroad, while the DHS is responsible for activity of the citizens whether inside or outside the borders of the U.S., with its stated goal, "to prepare for, prevent, and respond to domestic

[93] http://newsbusters.org/node/12556
[94] http://www.globalresearch.ca/dhs-constitution-free-zones-inside-us-ignored-by-media/5345308
[95] https://en.wikipedia.org/wiki/Fourth_Amendment_to_the_United_States_Constitution

emergencies, particularly terrorism." With more than 200,000 employees, the DHS is the third largest Cabinet department in the U.S. government. DHS constitutes a diverse merger of federal functions and responsibilities, incorporating 22 former government agencies into a single organization. DHS is headed by the Secretary of Homeland Security, who is <u>appointed</u> by the President of the United States with the consent of the United States Senate.[96] The Secretary serves at the pleasure of the President, making the agency (DHS) autonomous.

This discussion is not conspiratorial but is based in fact: The DHS has literally created an imaginary 'border' that engulfs the entire United States, out 100 miles from every single end of the nation. Within this fabricated 'border', the DHS can search your electronic belongings for no reason. We're talking about no suspicion; no reasonable cause whatsoever is required under their own regulations. The DHS is now above the Constitution and can operate under their own rules.[97] The level of unreported pure tyranny going on here is unprecedented.

Ayo Kimathi was the weapons and ammunition purchaser for the DHS, specifically for the U.S. Immigration and Customs Enforcement (ICE). As a DHS official, Kimathi's role at the agency was to procure guns and ammunition, of which the organization has purchased large quantities of both.[98]

It appears that government forces, specifically DHS, attempted to dry up the market by purchasing nearly all the ammunition that is produced, therefore causing panic buying in the private sector. The shortage blamed on the panic purchasing by private citizens. However, the real reason was government hoarding and the closing foreign ammunition markets which is setting the stage for the government to further its gun control ban with the U.N. Does it surprise anyone that cargo ships from Russia and foreign countries that also supply ammunition to U.S. markets

---

[96] *http://en.wikipedia.org/wiki/United_States_Department_of_Homeland_Security#Structure*
[97] *http://www.storyleak.com/dhs-constitution-free-zones-us/#ixzz2dEUWVXFF*
[98] *http://www.infowars.com/dhs-buys-1-6-billion-bullets*

were being forced to return to their home ports?[99] WHERE WAS ALL THE AMMUNITION GOING?

Mr. Kimathi has been cited for running a personal website "War on the Horizon," specifically espousing a racial war against all whites.[100] His website criticizes whites, gays, those of mixed race, and blacks who integrate with whites. Despite the inflammatory rhetoric, Mr. Kimathi, who is black, was eventually put on paid leave.[101] The Associated Press reported U.S. government officials were not immediately clear whether Kimathi crossed the legal threshold into unprotected hate speech, and the posts may not violate DHS policies if he does not post to the website at work or espouse the ideologies in the office. This twisted, illogical application of government rules and regulations can only occur when there is an agenda to protect. That agenda appeared to be the perpetuation of racial tension in the U.S. as a cover for the slow political, economic and physical destruction of our American way of life into a totalitarian dictatorship.

Is history repeating itself? In the article, *Nazification of Germany vs. Nazification of America*, by Norman D. Livergood, a once stable (pre 1933) Germany became socially and emotionally enamored by a relatively unknown German WWI veteran, Adolph Hitler. Hitler's infamous oratory skills won the hearts and minds of the German people by promising them a utopian society. Hitler convinced the German President Hindenburg to appoint the minority Nazi party as the dominant German political force and Hitler as chancellor. In short order, Hitler began immediately to orchestrate the complete takeover of all mechanisms of the governance and functions of state, to make Nazi Germany a totalitarian dictatorship. So similar are the comparison of 1933 Germany and present-day America, that a direct parallel is almost predictable.[102]

[99] http://beforeitsnews.com/international/2013/04/obama-signs-firearm-and-ammo-killswitch-2456326.html
[100] http://townhall.com/tipsheet/katiepavlich/2013/08/23/homeland-security-employee--has-a-website-dedicated-to-hating-white-people-n1671808
[101] http://www.huffingtonpost.com/2013/08/24/ayo-kimathi-paid-leave_n_3809450.html
[102] http://www.thirdworldtraveler.com/Fascism/Nazification_GermanyvsAmer.html

Additional Evidence of Government Overreach

Every government scandal has the implied benefit of interpretation by the very people who wrote the law. However, when that agenda gets applied to an individual in the private sector and not a government entity, it usually results in the destruction of the individual's personal character and livelihood. An example of such political outreach was the Paula Deen story. Deen has been physically, economically and emotionally destroyed by the "racist police" for alleged racially insensitive comments this southern Georgian girl made as far as 30 years prior, during a time when the "N" word didn't have the political "death wish" it has today. Certainly, Deen may not be the role model for the American image but she is an example of exercising her right to the American Dream. Deen made her millions consciously promoting morbid obesity. She was a Food Network star with corporate sponsorship by Target and Home Depot and even as a spokesperson for a pharmaceutical company's Diabetes drug which she herself has, in part caused by her reckless promotion of foods that enhance Diabetes.

To understand the connection between this story and the Progressive Agenda, one must look no further than Michelle Obama. The former first lady had taken on the mission (and legacy) of stopping morbid obesity, and especially in children. Could the political agenda of having the internet the media destroy Paula Deen, be complicit with Michelle Obama's war on obesity? I dare say that Paula Deen was hardly a household name but her success as an entrepreneur did go against the grain of the Progressive Agenda in terms of upholding the freedoms of the individual, let alone the affront to the First Lady's future legacy.

Paula Deen had the constitutional right to buck Michelle Obama's agenda but could the Obama administration's political machine have taken the opportunity of scoring a "two for one" victory by shutting down Deen's dynasty? When referring to the

Alinsky "bible" for a Progressive, Socialist takeover of a country, one could find an answer. Alinsky's Rule 5 states: "Ridicule is a man's most potent weapon, for which there is no defense." Rule 12 states: "Pick a target, cut off all support and go after the person not the institution."[103]

This story came to light when a complaint was made that this successful TV chef used the "N" word repeatedly in her past, and accusing Dean of being racist (Rule 5). Immediately following the racist story was the attack on what Dean did to gain her prominence and wealth; promoting obesity. What was once Deen's right to freedom of expression now became the enemy of the people: obesity.

Perhaps this story was not about Deen's personal character as it was about using her character in destroying an agenda opposed to what the First Lady couldn't accomplish on her own merit (Rule 12). Understanding the agenda of the progressive movement to move this country from its constitutional beginnings to a pre-planned government-controlled society, it is not a stretch for any administration to subliminally use the "race card" to destroy its enemies.

These scandals occurred since Jan 1, 2013. The idea is to push the public into information overload whereby resistance and due diligence goes down. As public scrutiny wanes the progressive agenda advances, until it's too late to find any semblance of our once free nation.

Secondary nonfederal government scandals were arising at the same time. Just to name one; look at the Red-Light safety cameras sweeping the country. The Chicago Tribune reported on March 3, 2013, that Chicago City Hall can't back up its claim of red-light cameras offering any beneficial safety.[104] Chicago voters were given nonexistent data to justify red light safety camera, supplied mostly by the camera's manufacturer. Illinois

[103] http://www.bestofbeck.com/wp/activism/saul-alinskys-12-rules-for-radicals
[104] http://articles.chicagotribune.com/2013-05-15/news/ct-met-inspector-general-red-light-cameras-0515-20130515_1_red-light-cameras-camera-program-new-speed-cameras

Inspector General Joe Ferguson had pointed out that the city has 389 red light cameras at 190 intersections. The cameras cost $25,000 a piece or $5.3 million and costs $13,800/yr. to maintain each camera. The scandal here lies in the reason for the cameras—they may not actually be intended to promote safety. The city wrote 612,278 tickets based on camera images, generating $72 million in revenue on a $5 million investment. Money talks!

However, the scandal may also lie in what these cameras provide for local and eventual any governmental entity based on recent invasion of privacy scandals within the Federal Government. Besides a windfall revenue stream, these cameras are public surveillance systems, providing license numbers, facial recognition technology and at the minimum an array of invasion of privacy functions. Naturally, city officials state no such data is collected; however, scandals abound given such untethered opportunity. The pacifying argument is, "If you are doing nothing wrong what does it matter?" The constitutional argument is our Bill of Rights and Constitutional Amendments were put in place to safeguard the citizens from the potential for government intrusion. We must always remember that with safety comes risk. To have safety without risk is the sign of a totalitarian environment, in which the population is willing to trade freedom for the perception of safety.

Outright executive lying to Congressional investigations has become the norm, with the "escape clause" being the use of executive privilege to circumvent prosecution. So it was in the case involving the "Fast & Furious" scandal, where some 1,400 firearms went into criminal hands to support rebel factions favorable to U.S. policies. Then Attorney General Eric Holder signed the order but refused to hand over documentation to congressional investigation. As a result, the House of Representatives found Holder in contempt of Congress, making him the first cabinet member in history to be held in contempt of Congress. The White House simply dismissed the congressional charges invoking Executive Privilege, thus legally side-stepping constitutional law.[105] This is not just government deception; this is government corruption.

Behind the scenes there is another deception taking place that will ultimately affect our two-party system of government. Our founding fathers were not interested in compromise, to the point of single mindedness, when it came to setting policy for this country. Modern day thinking is that our country is in trouble because Republican and Democrats can't agree on anything and if they only can agree to a single-minded focus, this country would resolve its issues. The premise of a two-party system is to bring diversity of thinking while minimizing the possibility of a tyrannical government takeover; a principle taught in every high school U.S. Government history 101 class. However, with common core education the norm in most states, historical reference to our founding principles is being lost.

If our two-party system of government essentially agrees on everything, then one party is expendable. A one-party system is comparable to types of government such as a monarchy or at worst a dictatorship. Without our viable two-party systems, how long would it take for the next Hitler or Caligula to attain power? It took but 6 months for the Roman Emperor Caligula to rule the Roman Empire as a tyrant, perverting Roman civilization into utter chaos with only his death by assassination saving the empire.

Without educating our youth to the responsibilities associated with freedom and ensuring historical significance to the genius of our founding fathers, our government officials will vie for personal power and wealth at the expense of the people. A good example of government officials vying for power, presented itself within the Republican Party over the emergence of the Tea Party, which was formed by concerned citizens and government officials.

---

[105] http://articles.latimes.com/2012/jun/20/news/la-pn-obama-invokes-executive-privilege-over-fast-and-furious-documents-20120620

On October 7, 2013, Senate Republican Minority leader Mitch McConnell called a private meeting of all Republican senators behind closed doors. After the meeting, the senators were sworn to secrecy due to the sensitivity of the topic and relevance to the future of the Republican Party. However, it wasn't long before the content of the meeting was leaked to key conservative news agencies, oddly enough not by the conservative constitutionalist Tea Party advocates within the Republican Party, but by the more progressive middle of the road republicans, more aligned with traditional democratic progressive views. The message was clear; Senator Mitch McConnell was furious that the potential future rival for his Republican Kentucky Senate seat, businessman and entrepreneur conservative Mathew Bevin had bought airtime to disclose backroom dealings with the progressive agenda including pressuring Republican Senators not to join the effort to defund Obamacare.[106] Senator Mitch McConnell had utter distain for the conservative "Tea Party" republicans that threaten McConnell's power base.

The meeting was simple and direct. McConnell announced that any republican senator that disagrees with his decisions in moving the republican party away from the conservative movement will be considered an enemy of his and the country. McConnell called out freshman senators like Ted Cruz, Marco Rubio, Mike Lee and Rand Paul because of their opposition to his decisions and their "constitutionalist" opposition to the progressive movement.[107]

Politics can be a dirty game but under the U.S. constitution, the brilliance of the founding fathers can be admired. Our constitution essentially protects the people from a potential tyrannical takeover of our government. It is the will of the people that sends representative to the U.S. government. It is the job of these representatives to represent the very will of the citizens who elected them. It wasn't difficult to see that our government was operating according to its own agenda alerting

---

[106] *http://www.huffingtonpost.com/2014/03/09/mitch-mcconnell-tea-party_n_4930160.html*
[107] *http://www.businessinsider.com/mitch-mcconnell-crush-conservative-insurgents-2014-3*

some of our elected U.S. government officials that "something is afoul." The birth of the Tea Party was being portrayed as the radical fringe when in fact, just the opposite is true. The Tea Party was never meant to be a rival 3rd party to our system of government but an attempt to secure a non-progressive stronghold for the Republican or Democratic Party.

The democratic party, led by Harry Reid, Nancy Pelosi and President Obama had made it clear by their actions that the "will of the people be damned." It was the Tea Party constitutionalists that attempted to bring this government back to its founding principles. Is it any wonder that such turmoil now exists within our own government? On one hand the constitutionalists (former Tea Party) are not the radicals but the "norm" that this country was founded upon. On the other hand, nearly 100 years of continual subversive actions have occurred that has led to the incredible accomplishment of making both the Democratic and Republican parties essentially one party posing as two. It is impossible to ignore the facts any longer, no matter what your political affiliation.

Has it ever occurred to anyone just how our constitutional government can totally ignore some of the most incredible breaches of trust in U.S. history? Have you noticed that absolutely nothing was done to punish or rectify the IRS scandal whereby ONLY conservative political groups and certain ordinary citizens were targeted for audit or denial of their nonprofit status without cause? Have you also noticed that nothing has yet been done to date about the DOJ and FBI lies perpetrated against congress and the FISA court about the Steele dossier? Where is the outrage over the Benghazi incident, where a U.S. Ambassador and several other U.S. staffers were killed in the U.S. consulate under the false flag of an anti-Muslim video? Why has this event slipped from any news coverage? Where are the investigations by either party?

There is audio proof in 2006 containing then Senator Obama and then Senate Majority leader Harry Reid openly going on record calling out President Bush for attempting to even think about raising the debt ceiling above 10 trillion dollars, rather than control reckless spending. They even stated that it is unconscionable to lay that kind of debt on future generations. Wouldn't it seem a simple matter of Republicans buying airtime to just play the audio before the American public? Why was this not even discussed?

The answer lies in the fact that there is neither an attempt to chase down these scandals nor solve the debt crisis, other than the initial puffery to appear concerned. Make no mistake, present Democratic law makers are tenured to force the people of this country into total dependence on Progressive government doctrine. As this country was slowly slipping into an unrecognizable entity, it was the hope of the Progressive movement in Congress, to induce a "checkmate" scenario on U.S. citizens where, by the time they realize what constitutional freedoms have been lost, there will be no hope to recover. Fortunately, our democratic republic can self-correct every four years, as we are witnessing under the present Trump administration.

Compliance is the necessary tool of tyranny. Compliance at the end of a gun barrel is Communism; compliance at the end of entitlement programs is Socialism, compliance to political and social theories is Marxism, compliance to customer satisfaction is Capitalism. The reason Capitalism works, and all other political and economic models are doomed to failure is that Capitalism removes the need for a big centralized government, thus minimizing the possibility of tyrannical influence. The failure of Capitalism will only come at the hands of ordinary citizens unwilling to maintain their constitutional rights of individual responsibility as delineated by the Bill of Rights.

The U.S. has the power to pick and choose its elected officials. There are 535 members of congress (100 senators and 435 members of the House of Representatives) charged with representing the ideology of the people. Senators are elected for a 6 year term with 1/3rd of the senior Senators up for re-election every two years, whereas each member of the House of Representatives serves a two year term in order to provide access to the best suited for the task and for the removal of congressional representatives that are not fulfilling their obligation. With that said, how then do ineffective, separate agenda driven or outright unlawful members of congress get elected and reelected despite their destructive and at times, illegal activities?

The answer lies in the voting process itself. One man, one vote, was the way to give equal representation to all legal citizens that have a stake in matters of country. Voting requires participation by all. When one chooses to not vote, he is in fact voting. Voting records in cities like New York, where vast pockets of influential people reside are notorious for their "groupie" type voter behavior. Whether for self-interests or political pandering, once a large number of voters obtains the influence to convince the other voters that it is futile to resist their will at the ballot box, complacency overrides their constitutional responsibility. Once complacency becomes the norm, the seeds for tyranny have been sown.

Capitol Hill Blue, the oldest political news site on the internet, revealed that 29 members of Congress have been accused of spousal abuse; 7 have been arrested for fraud, 19 have been accused of writing bad checks, 117 have bankrupted at least two businesses, 3 have been arrested for assault, 71 have credit reports so bad they can't qualify for a credit card, 8 have been arrested for shoplifting, 21 are current defendants in lawsuits. The Capitol Hill Blue also reported that in 1998 alone, 84 were stopped for drunk driving, but released after they claimed Congressional immunity, noting that some were "serial offenders" with extensive tracks records of fraud or violence.

Former Representative Corrine Brown (D-FL) had a "long, consistent record of deceit," including tens of thousands of dollars in unpaid bills, allegations of bribery, and numerous lawsuits against her. Members of Congress routinely bankrupt businesses, write bad checks, engage in fraudulent practices, and have bad credit.[108] Perhaps that can be a clue as to why our country is carrying a national debt of 22 trillion dollars and why federal programs are always over budget and wasteful. Given the economic incompetence of so many Senators and Representatives, you must wonder why voters trust them with a budget to run the country. It is interesting to note that one of the platforms of our present Trump administration espoused was "draining the swamp," a brilliant visual for a political system in need of an overhaul.

Steve Dasbach, former national director of the Libertarian Party stated: "are these really the kind of economically illiterate people we want to trust with our money?" Mr. Dasbach also stated that "If nothing else, the Capitol Hill Blue investigation may help puncture the myth that Senators and Representatives are somehow superior to ordinary Americans, or better equipped to solve the nation's problems." "By its very nature, politics tends to attract venal people who crave power, who want to control the lives of other people, and who think they are above the law."[109]

One of the most glaring examples of voter negligence is Representative Charles B. Rangel of New York, who has been re-elected into office 20 consecutive times since 1973. The issue is not his time in office but his dismal record of accomplishments as well as his extensive record of Ethics and Censure violations. In a Wikipedia article on Rangel, it states: "In July 2008, The Washington Post reported that Rangel was soliciting donations to the Charles B. Rangel Center for Public Service at City College of New York from corporations with business interests before in his Ways and Means Committee and did so using Congressional letterhead.[110] Rangel rented Harlem apartments he owned at below-market rates, illegally receiving thousands of dollars in campaign funds from landlord kickback, while using one apartment as a clandestine campaign office. Rangel had been using a House of Representative parking garage as

[108] http://web.archive.org/web/20000229050220/www.capitolhillblue.com/Aug1999/081699/cr
[109] http://termlimits.com/best.htm
[110] http://en.wikipedia.org/wiki/Charles_B._Rangel#2008.E2.80.932010:_Ethics_issues_and_censure

free storage space for his Mercedes-Benz for years, in violation of Congressional rules. Rangel faced tax evasion for failing to report income from his $1,100/night rental beachside villa he owns in Punta Cana in the Dominican Republic as well as from the sale of his $500,000 home Washington D.C., and income from investment fund reporting.

Rangel has blatantly ignored the rule of law by hiding behind congressional privilege, yet he is re-elected at each election. The reason is simple, his loyal voters and benefactors of his mischievous behavior show up in mass at each election, while the rest of his district stays home knowing they can't do anything to unseat him; a classic miscarriage of constitutional responsibilities.

In comparison, what is the penalty for an average citizen who steals one stamp from a post office? The "United States Post Office is a federal operation; it would be a federal crime which can result in incarceration in a federal prison for at least 1 year. Federal prisoners serve every day of their sentence; no time off for good behavior."[111]

The voting record and personal activities of congressional officials are public record. Under our constitution, it is perfectly legal to be stupid or incompetent however, do we need stupid or incompetent people running our government, or worse controlling the activities of our lives? Once in violation of congressional rules, your tenure should be over, held to no higher standard of ethics that an average citizen. In the U.S., congressional tenure is terminated at the ballot box. How unconscionable, for an elected official, to force its electorate into servitude when they themselves are guilty of electoral prostitution and illegal behavior. Only complacency and the willingness to give up your right of freedom of choice, so vehemently secured for us by our founding fathers, can an out of control government continue to prosper.

[111] http://en.wikipedia.org/wiki/Federal_crime

For Further Reading

Answers Corporation. "How Many US Senators and Congressmen Are Convicted Felons?" WikiAnswers. http://wiki.answers.com/Q/How_many_US_senators_and_congressmen_are_convicted_felons (accessed July 17, 2014).

Benson, Bill, and M. J. Beckman. *The law that never was: the fraud of the 16th Amendment and personal income tax*. South Holland, IL (Box 550, South Holland 60473): Constitutional Research Assoc., 1985.

"COMMON CORE." COMMON CORE. http://whatiscommoncore. wordpress.com (accessed July 16, 2014).

Sothern, Marci. "Responsibilities of the Federal Government." eHow. http://www.ehow.com/list_7654222_responsibilities-federal-government.html#ixzz2wE9vPYin (accessed July 16, 2014).

Wikimedia Foundation. "Patriot Act." Wikipedia. http://en. wikipedia.org/wiki/Patriot_Act (accessed July 16, 2014).

YouTube. "Gun Myths Gone in Five Minutes: ABC News 20/20." YouTube. https://www.youtube.com/watch?v=682JLrsUmEM (accessed July 17, 2014).

Zieve, Sher. "Behind Common Core: Forcing Marxism/Nazism on America's Children." GulagBoundcom. http://gulagbound. com/38714/common-core-forcing-marxismnazism-on-americas-children/ (accessed July 16, 2014).

CHAPTER FOUR

WHAT DOES IT ALL MEAN?

T he problem with information is that it can ramble, become disjointed and lose its effectiveness if it is not organized properly. What is happening to our country is a complicated story based on secrecy, deception and disinformation. So convoluted is the trail of events, that to the average person, when confronted with the truth, is denial and even dismissal.

This reaction by the average American can be described as incredulous and is precisely the reason that the events which are dismantling our country can be hidden in plain sight. I've spent over a decade piecing together the events and inconsistencies in current national and international events, knowing that somewhere there are others doing the same thing. I have been fortunate in traveling and meeting people with vital, firsthand information that not only verifies my personal research but lends insights into a deeper world I have yet to discover.

As of this writing, one such source has come to light that has altered my thinking by giving structure, facts and references necessary to "put the pieces together" with confidence. Foster Gamble, a Princeton University graduate and heir to the Proctor & Gamble corporation, spent most of his life in the pursuit of energy sources known to world history but never utilized due to corporate and governmental suppression.[112] In his free DVD *THRIVE*[113] documentation and solutions are revealed that will instill confidence and insight into what "we the people" can do

---

[112] *http://thrivedoucmentaryreview.blogspot.com/2011/11/about-foster-gamble.html*
[113] *http://m.thrivemovement.com/#watch*

stop the progressive takeover and the eventual destruction of our country.

I will devote the rest of this chapter to summarize the events that have changed our world and the solutions already in play to stop the onslaught; however, this is not a substitute for firsthand recognition and analysis. Although repetition of some events and stories may occur, understand that hearing about these events as they unfold from different perspectives, only adds emphasis to their meaning.

The problem we are presently facing is that the creativity of our species has been stifled by controlling forces that have succeeded in altering every aspect of our lives without our consent or knowledge. It can be said that an elite group of people and corporations that control all our energy, food and water supplies, education and healthcare, control our lives.

My remarks in the Introduction stated that what we are now experiencing began with the 1910 secret meeting on Jekyll Island, where seven of the most important families in banking, corporate and international commerce, met to form a "New World Order." The outcome of that meeting is the basis of all that we are experiencing today. The following are the areas of civilization most controlled by the New World Order agenda.

Note: the analysis that follows was in place long before the Trump Presidency. The elimination of burdensome and needless government regulations by the Trump Administration has allowed the U.S. to become a net exporter of energy; however, the analysis below is still accurate in terms of "New World Order" dominance.

Energy

The U.S. can be totally self-sufficient with its vast untapped reserves of coal, oil and natural gas from fracking, yet we are dependent on foreign energy supplies. The reason is simple: U.S. energy corporations can control prices on imported energy, discouraging venture capital investing in our own natural resources. Numerous other factors exist creating an illusion of energy shortages, but this is not the forum for such discussion.

Civilizations have long understood the geometric principles of the "Torus" configuration and its relationship to "perfect energy." The Torus shows us how energy moves in its most balanced dynamic flow process. The simplest description of its overall form is that of a donut, where energy flows through a central axis, adapting to environmental challenges.[114] There have been numerous "free" energy developments eventually leading to the discovery of the Torus "free" energy field. The problem was that these discoveries went against the controlling corporate forces reaping in the 200 trillion-dollar oil and nuclear power industries. Profits from oil prices produce enough money to suppress any alternative energy threat to the Rockefeller (Standard Oil) petroleum and agriculture industry.

Energy is the fundamental backbone of society. Ancient civilizations had incredible knowledge of how energy is created and used it to produce projects like the pyramids of Giza in Egypt, Machu Picchu in Peru and structures that cannot be duplicated with today's advanced technology. John Hutchison, a Canadian inventor who studied the works of engineer Nikola Tesla, developed an anti-gravity device that taps into the "free energy" of the universe.[115] His labs were raided by U.S. government officials and his work destroyed. In 1991, Dr. Eugene Mallove developed a safe cold fusion energy source available to anyone. He stated and proved that one gallon of water was equal to 300 gallons of gasoline with his cold fusion technology. The established scientific research of the day was funded to produce dangerous thermonuclear fusion power. Dr. Mallove was mysteriously murdered and his work disappeared and lab destroyed.[116] Adam Trombly is a scientist with years of

[114] 234 http://www.cosmometry.net/the-torus---dynamic-flow-process
[115] http://rationalwiki.org/wiki/John Hutchison
[116] http://en.wikipedia.org/wiki/Eugene Mallove

experience as an inventor working with game changing energy and geophysical technologies. He developed a levitation power source.[117] His work was ridiculed by established scientists and his lab and files mysteriously burnt to the ground.

Education

The agenda of the Rockefeller, Ford and Carnegie Foundations is to produce a docile work force through a mandatory education system designed around reflexive responses, thwarting independent thinking and competition. Independent thinking is not highly regarded. Initial 46 states had adopted the Common Core State Standards to be compliant with government standards and funding. It wasn't long before the flaws (agenda) in the Common Core Curriculum became apparent. At least 12 states have since introduced legislation to repeal the standards; 4 or which have totally withdrawn. There are 2 main reasons for concern: states are losing their constitutional right to determine the educational standards for their particular state, using government funding as the 'carrot' and the Common Core Curriculum falls short on historical reference while virtually discouraging ANY parental involvement in their child's educational experience.

Medicine

The American Medical Association is a Rockefeller-controlled entity sponsored almost entirely by the corporate-friendly National Dairy Council, Beef.org, American Sugar Alliance, pharmaceutical and other sponsors. The result is that medical doctors are trained from a pharmaceutical perspective and have only one course in nutrition with texts that are supplied by the research of corporate sponsors. Deepak Chopra, MD, states: "medical schools are funded by pharmaceutical industry, with the motive to sell drugs not health." Reality is that pharmaceuticals are designed to treat

---

[117] *http://www.venusproject.org/new-energy/free-energy-device-demonstration-adam-trombly.html*

(as opposed to solve) the problem, thus perpetuating the problem it was intended to eliminate via side effects of the drug.

Controlling forces suppress "true cures" the same as it suppresses alternative free energy. Dr. Royal Rife developed a Frequency Resonance Generator capable of destroying cancer cells and viruses. His generators were tested on 16 terminal cancer patients over a three-month period. The result was a 100% cure rate. Shortly thereafter, his entire lab was destroyed by fire and his research records lost. While trying to recover, Dr. Rife was faced with defending numerous frivolous and expensive lawsuits by "paid for hire" medical doctors who destroyed Dr. Rife financially. Others like Dr. Max Gerson and Harry Hoxsey also had formulations that "cured" cancer through specific food nutraceuticals (foods that heal) but the AMA vilified them with trumped up charges and rigged independent testing, showing no significant value to their work.[118, 119] Currently, countries outside the U.S. are using their formulas with incredible success, drawing people with the means to travel out of the country with near complete recoveries.

On a personal note, a terminally ill cancer patient with less than 6 months to live, left the U.S. to treat with the Gerson protocols in Mexico. One year later he returned to my office completely cured of cancer, now helping others understand the Gerson protocols outside the U.S. Unless the pharmaceutical industry can patent a product or technology for a cure, it will never see the light of day.

What the pharmaceutical industry never anticipated was interference via the executive branch of the Federal Government; ie, the President. On May 22, 2018, congress passed President Trump's "Right to Try Act," fulfilled his promise to expand healthcare options for terminally ill Americans. The bill amends Federal law to allow certain FDA unapproved or experimental drugs to be administered to terminally ill patients who have exhausted all approved treatment options and are unable to participate in clinical drug trials. The "Right to Try" legislation

[118] http://www.healingcancernaturally.com/medical-history.html
[119] http://gersontreatment.com/if-it-is-so-good-why-havent-i

returns treatment decisions back to patients, giving them the right to make healthcare choices that could save their lives.[120]

Similarly, the pharmaceutical industry and their paid lobbyists have long pushed the narrative that ALL children must be vaccinated, for their own safety and the safety of society. Vaccines are under great scrutiny by prominent scientists, to ensure safety and efficacy because of the unreported harm caused by non-medicinal ingredients. (*See earlier chapter, "Health Care and The Medicine Man"*) President Trump has instituted The Department for Conscious and Religious Freedom also given new hope for parents of those children caught in the medical cabal having to participate in ALL vaccine programs or not being able to participate society via the Gestapo tactics of HHS, CDC, FDA, who have effectively silenced the voices of scientists and medical doctors with opposing data. "The chemicals found in vaccines cause autism, period. The only people and organizations that say otherwise are paid to say so. We know the truth and we will not vaccinate our children to death!" Dr. Alvin H Moss, MD, Nephrologist, West Virginia University.[121]

The Automobile Industry

Germany designed and perfected the Wankel Rotary Engine and introduced it to the auto industry in 1964. It was a three-sided rotary combustion chamber that can develop extremely high RPM, incredible fuel economy, low cost and was as close to a perpetual motion machine as possible (in terms of wear and tear). Various auto manufacturers bid on the engine, but it was Mazda who put it into production. GM eventually bought the patent from Mazda, then created controversy over production problems and basically buried the patient (and the engine). Clearly, this was done to stop any challenge to traditional gas-guzzling piston engines. With ever rising oil and gasoline prices, people looked to foreign auto manufacturers for fuel efficient,

---

[120] *https://www.whitehouse.gov/briefings-statements/president-donald-j-trump-sign-right-try-legislation-fulfilling-promise-made-expand-healthcare-options-terminal-americans/*
[121] *https://www.sorightithurts.com/2019/01/05/trump-signs-order-vaccines-no-longer-required-for-children*

less expensive automobiles. The market shift hurt American auto manufacturers resulting in government support in the form of massive bailout windfalls to GM and Chrysler; most of which went to the corporate elite that financially supported the progressive Democratic Party as recognition for their continued support. Almost none of the 80 billion dollars to GM and Chrysler was allocated for its intended "job saving" use. Today, GM is once again headed for bankruptcy.

Economy

The formation of the Federal Reserve System is comprised of privately-owned corporations that answer to no one and have nothing to do with the government or its banking system. David Icke described the Ponzi scheme of the Federal Reserve: "You get a bank loan. The bank puts a number representing money into your account. You immediately begin to pay interest totaling 3X the loan value on money that never really existed other than a computer entry. This is called 'Fractional Banking,' meaning that the Federal Reserve can loan 9X the value of your loan to other banks making loans, knowing that the interest will reap huge financial rewards."[122]

Loaning fictitious money is the printing of fiat money (simply put it is the printing of money from thin air). Banks therefore can loan nine dollars for every one dollar it receives, and they make a whopping 90% profit on all loans. Fractional Banking was the product of the Jekyll Island meeting in 1913 and served as the part of the founding principles for the formation of the Federal Reserve System.

Politicians, knowing how this system worked, quickly formed alliances with the supporters of this independent banking cartel called the Federal Reserve. In return, the Federal Reserve, with help from member banks, prints Fiat money to be used by politicians for their pet programs, often without congressional approval or the support of the people they represent.

[122] https://www.youtube.com/watch?v=R8f826BX6po

It should be no surprise that the IRS was also formally established in 1913, essentially taxing the people on their personal income to pay politicians and the Federal debt. To this day there is no accounting for the "slush fund" created by the IRS but instead gives the illusion of using the money to run the government.

To the extreme, 2008-2011 represented the largest printing of fiat money in the history of the U.S., disguised as bailouts to major corporations for the purpose of stimulating jobs. The extreme economic pressure presented by the printing of this historic amount of fiat currency caused the devaluation of the real estate market. The devaluation of property forced people to default on their government-owned loans; some of which were underwritten by the government-owned mortgage companies Freddie Mac and Fanny Mae; making the government the owner of a windfall of devalued property. When the time arrives to give the illusion of economic recovery, the government can now resell the property and reap the entire new values of the properties under the same Fractional Banking system of mortgage loans, thus completing the "rape" of the private property of citizens. To date, any attempt to expose any unconstitutional government activity is met with swift FBI raids, usually on trumped up charges that take years to unravel; long enough to bankrupt the offending entity while destroying its credibility in the media.

Just 16 years after the historic 1913 Jekyll Island meeting, the first step in the master global plan to bring all countries into a "New World Order" was implemented. By 1929 the U.S. was in its biggest boom economy ever. Money was invested in internal growth projects as well as in the stock market, supporting companies with the technology and manpower to provide wealth and independence to the people. However, much of the stock market was supported by the continual influx of money from the banking cartels, often providing money to companies, simply to prop the stock market. On that fateful day in 1929, these same banking cartels suddenly and without warning pulled their money from the market, causing a catastrophic panic selling of stocks by the middle class and a crash in stock values. The stock market crash of 1929 marked the beginning of the Great Depression and the visual success of the elite in implementing their grand plan.

After many years of stock devaluation, these same banking cartels began to buy back the same stocks at pennies on the dollar; only this time as partners in these corporations and not just investors. The grand government scheme was to first cause a problem then become the *solution* to the problem. To the astute observer, this same scenario has played out many times over the years, the last taking place in the real estate crash of 2008.

To summarize how this scheme works:

1. The member Federal Reserve Banks put out loans at low interest rates, creating the illusion of a boom economy.

2. The Federal Reserve raises the interest rates to the point that people become over extended and upside down on their loans.

3. Companies go out of business; wages and jobs drop drastically.

4. Bankruptcy and short sales take over property at highly devalued amounts.

5. Banks put money back into the economy, giving the illusion of a recovery, and the process repeats itself.

The diversion tactic used is to keep the people busy by creating a continued source of class warfare, immigration, racial tension, terrorism, threatening the disappearing of entitlements and even the diversion of court activity recently seen in the Zimmerman/

Trayvon Martin fiasco. It's the old carnival shell game of misguided distraction. Make no mistake; world domination culminating in a New World Order is the agenda, which requires total control and domination of the essentials of any civilization. There are six major areas of society targeted by the elite controlling class:

- **Money:** The central banks such as the Federal Reserve System, International Monetary Fund and the World Bank, all controlled by the banking cartel families of the world.

- **Energy:** Complete control over Oil, Natural Gas, Coal and Nuclear Energy. The development of "free" or "natural energy" sources are totally forbidden and intentionally undermined even when it seems otherwise to the public. The government bailout of Solyndra, a solar energy company, was a perfect example. Huge sums of money were funneled into Solyndra by the Federal Reserve, similar to the Freddie Mac mortgage scheme. The government also made sure Solyndra received no contracts, therefore ensuring its demise and furthering the myth that viable alternative energy sources are not practicable.

- **Food & Water:** The World Trade m Organization is buying up world water sources under the guise of standardizing the purity of drinking water. Under Codex Alimentarius (international food laws), world governments would have the authority to make water a pharmaceutical grade entity, thus requiring scripts.

- **Healthcare:** The pharmaceutical industry funds most of our medical schools' costs. They also fund the textbook selection and the curriculum, ensuring only "drugs" will be taught. The AMA is not at arm's length with the pharmaceutical industry—it's joined at the hip. Medical students receive only one cursory course in nutrition and learn nothing about alternative healthcare.

- **Information:** The elite class insures a standard, compulsory education entirely centered around "reflexive" learning where learning is on a "need to know" basis. The media receives most of its operating money and licenses to broadcast providing they project the story lines that the elite agenda wants people to see and believe. Progressives within the NWO are working hard to find ways to control the presently uncontrolled internet, under the guise of public safety or military need.

- **Control Descent:** The Patriot Act is working, even as it is supported by trading our freedoms for security. Terror is the means to circumvent constitutional laws. The executive branch of government is granting itself the power to stop and search without warrant if there is suspicion of terrorist activity. That person can even be held in prison indefinitely without due process. Surveillance cameras track our every move, under the silly notion of traffic control.

Seven families and their corporations seem to have control over every aspect of our civilization. They are the Rothschilds, Rockefellers, Morgans, Schiffs, Warburgs, Carnegies and Harrimans. Their goal is not about money but about power and control over the world. To them, freedom is dangerous in the hands of the common man; therefore they need to control people for their own good. Their divide and conquer tactic is put into play by instigating eternal infighting between the races, Republicans and Democrats, and the haves and the have-nots. They believe the only source of supreme power is a military dictatorship run by a world power like the U.N. Our nation has witnessed this as recently as the Iraq war, where our military generals at times answered to a United Nations peace keeping force.

Discovering the truth about the world domination agenda is written off as conspiracy theory. Making a public spectacle or court action against such individuals discourages others from doing the same. The whistle- blower Edward Snowden is in the throes of such government activity. Whether his actions were good or evil, he discovered the truth during a time he was trained to do otherwise. Are his actions that of a traitor or an unsung hero? Only time will tell.

World Domination does not come easily once the game is revealed. The special forces of the elite class are the Illuminati and the FBI. These highly secret organizations dictate what the societal norms are. If you live according to their norms, then you are normal. If you step out of their box, you are considered to be a radical, racist, conspirator or traitor and must be stopped. The result is that people would choose to comply, rather than confront.

To further implement the agenda of world domination, the New World Order has broken down the globe into manageable unions. To date there is the European Union, African Union, Pacific Union and as soon as the U.S. falls in line, the American Union. These unions are totally dominated and controlled by the World Trade Organization, World Health Organization and the World Bank.

It was *Confessions of an Economic Hitman* author John Perkins who revealed the method of creating manageable territorial unions. The plan is for the World Government to go into countries and offer huge infrastructure, medical, educational or social project loans designed to help bring these countries into the modern age. When they agree, vast sums of money are allocated to these countries, however the money actually goes to American corporations of the Elite class (such as Bechtel, Halliburton, GM, GE and others), who build the projects and reap the profits.[123] The result is that these countries get few benefits from the programs but are responsible for paying back the entire loan with interest. Knowing these countries can never repay these loans, the world powers instead make a

---

[123] *http://www.bookrags.com/studyguide-confessions-of-an-economic-hit-man*

deal. If these countries elect presidents favorable to New World Order agendas, the debt is forgiven. If they do not comply the presidents are ousted, killed or made into international villains like Osama Bin Laden and Saddam Hussein, both former allies of the western world that outlived their usefulness.

The real question is after all these years, how do these world dominators keep their agendas a secret? They do so by structuring their hierarchy on a strict "need to know" basis. Power is structured in tiers such that each tier doesn't know what their superior tier is doing, until only a precious few at the top tier know the complete truth. This leads to secrecy by "implied deniability," where nobody really knows the entire picture.

At this point in the New World Order's evolution, only the U.S. stands in their way. The push is on to bring down the U.S. economically. It must be noted that the plan is working to perfection. The U.S. is presently 16 trillion dollars in debt for the record but the actual number may be many times more when factoring in unfunded liabilities like Medicare and Medicaid and government pensions. The U.S. presently borrows more than 40 cents of every dollar to pay its debts and prints a good portion of the remainder via the Federal Reserve. This debt is collapsing all six areas of control necessary for take-over. If left to completion, the NWO will have stolen all productivity and wealth of this nation and move it into their international banking system.

The U.S. is moving closer to an insurmountable debt by design. The only way to solve the problem is to move into a "currency-less" monetary system where "push button" economics takes over. This allows the NWO banking system to literally remove or steal the wealth of an individual or corporation at the push of a button as was witnessed recently in Greece.

To do so requires a major distraction from reality. Global disasters provide such stimulus. At the latest G8 summit, the following was discussed: a "global tax" to combat global warming, a tax on CO_2 emissions and Cap-and-Trade regulations based on environmental criteria. The talks were to produce a global tax paid to the World Bank, enforced by a World Military Police Force.

To make this happen the controllers for world domination need a world crisis or the fear of terrorism on U.S. soil. Time and again our country has been faced with occurrences that defy understanding. The occurrence of 9/11 gave such a circumstance. With all of our intelligence and safeguards, somehow four jet liners slipped through our national defenses, with two achieving direct hits in the middle of New York City. The result was four buildings taken down, 2,996 lives lost and setting up a "who done it" lasting nearly 10 years which succeeded in bringing on the era of TERRORISM to the U.S.[124]

Post-Vietnam, the then Secretary of Defense, Robert McNamara, admitted that the U.S. entered the war under the false pretense that a U.S. ship was torpedoed in the Gulf of Tonka, triggering a swift U.S. military action.[125] The incident never occurred but the diversion of war deflected attention from the controlling forces.

The Iraq war was entered under the premise of confirmed Weapons of Mass Destruction, hidden by Saddam Hussein in the deserts of Iraq. Weapons of Mass Destruction were never found but the war continued long enough to again deflect the true agenda of the NWO. The Afghan war was a mere carry-over of the Iraq war where no clear objective was ever established but the continuation of a decade of distraction and the draining of vital economic resources, let alone the loss of life.

Keep in mind that comments made here are not to trivialize, disrespect or compromise any of these events but to point out their usefulness to world dominating forces. Often times these sinister groups instigate warring factions, then financially

[124] *http://www.statisticbrain.com/911-death-statistics*
[125] *http://www.examiner.com/article/war-under-false-pretenses-and-owning-up-to- the-truth*

support both sides of the conflict for the sole purpose of extending its usefulness.

Each of these events was continually furthered by fictitious stories fed to the media by our government, acting as their personal PR firm. Trial by media ensued, fanning the flames of terrorism and the relentless hunt for Osama and Saddam; both ending in "death to the tyrants" as the story lines came to a close. I personally found the killing of Osama bin Laden lacking the intellectual responsibility for closure. After a decade of hunting, we hear about the killing of Osama and the immediate removal of his body to an aircraft carrier for "proper sea burial" . . . proper sea burial? When has the Navy buried anyone at sea lately, let alone an enemy combatant under the guise of respecting strict Muslim law . . . huh? Without photographic evidence, identification other than the military's word or proof of any sort, this event is almost impossible to believe after ten years of anticipation. Such an incident defies logic, would never happen under normal conditions but is necessary for controlling forces to keep a bewildered population off balance.

Fear is the next criterion that ensures compliance. Create events like the Swine Flu or the Bird Flu epidemic. Create stories with reasonable believability. Have the media whip the population into frenzy. Have the government provide a solution, in the form of a vaccine and force the population to stampede health centers. Once established as a successful campaign, repeat the fear tactic again and again until the population simply stops questioning the events and relies on the creators of the epidemics to provide the solution. The swine flu and bird flu epidemic never occurred but leaves the public questioning whether the next epidemic is real or not. Surveillance is key to a successful world domination campaign.

Unbeknownst to the population, our driver's licenses and passports are printed with tracking chips to potentially follow our every move.[126, 127] Cameras are everywhere and

[126] http://www.wanttoknow.info/microchippassport
[127] http://www.offthegridnews.com/2013/09/09/drivers-license- chips- soon-will-allow-government-to-track-you

GPS technology in our cell phones insure accurate tracking. Facebook and social media have opened the door to data gathering on a massive voluntary scale. Even our healthcare records may soon by implanted in our bodies via chips to ensure accurate medical access.

Hundreds of FEMA detention camps have been set up on government owned lands for times of pandemics or civil unrest. However, the most sinister cornerstone to the global agenda is to lessen the population of the world dramatically via forced sterilization.[128] Much of what took place in 1940s Germany was the byproduct of the Carnegie Institute for Eugenics and the Rockefeller Population Council, which laid the blueprint for deciding who should live or die based on genetic or social traits.[129] Present day attempts at eugenics goes under the program of Chem Trails, where entire cities are sprayed from the air with unknown agents capable of producing disease and infertility, all in plain sight and never mentioned by an investigative media.

The U.S. has been testing vaccines and toxic substances on the military since WW2 without ever notifying the recipient in any way. The military men and women are chattel property of the government and as such have very little say as to what happens to them.

In this time of economic and basic philosophical transformation our country is experiencing, the work of Ayn Rand's 1957 book, *Atlas Shrugged*, again comes to mind. This truth-filled story portrays what happens when government entities go astray as well as what happens when people are oppressed by activists who are hell-bent on changing society and the economy to meet their agenda. So similar are the underlying themes in Atlas Shrugged to our present economic and political situation that it appeared Ayn Rand was writing about present day society. The lessons of *Atlas Shrugged* should serve as a blueprint for the

---

[128] *http://www.prisonplanet.com/the-population-reduction-agenda-for-dummies.html*
[129] *http://www.sfgate.com/opinion/article/Eugenics-and-the-Nazis-the-California-2549771.php*

recovery of our country. It takes courage to fight in the face of adversity; it also takes a plan.

Time will tell if the lessons of *Atlas Shrugged* and the genius of our founding fathers will prevail or not. Until that time, the clock is ticking!

CHAPTER FIVE

HOW WILL HISTORY JUDGE PRESIDENT OBAMA?

E arly in his presidency, President Obama talked about the Constitution as the basis of bringing back the traditions of our nation's founding. However, what has transpired are implementations of major social programs, Obama care and executive order legislation without bipartisan consult or congressional consensus—hardly our founding principles. Obama care is a prime example of bypassing constitutional law. All bills must originate in the House of Representatives, Obama care was not likely to reach legislative status since the House was controlled by republicans. Instead Obama implemented "sleight of hand" politics to bypass congressional oversight.

Another example of this appeared when Obama was not able to obtain congressional approval, even from moderate Democrats, on limiting CO_2 emissions and other environmental goals. By executive order the Obama administration used the Food and Drug Administration to present written regulations imposing new and onerous requirements on business; standards that could either destroy the businesses or force them into non-compliance and subsequent penalty taxes. The Food and Drug Administration (FDA) is an appointed agency of the U.S. Department of Health and Human Services, one of the United States federal executive departments, which essentially answers to no one except the president. With emboldened tactics, Obama openly stated that if congress stands in the way of his decisions, he can simply do it anyway.

Obama and his hard-left agenda required him to treat the Constitution and Congress as an inconvenience, standing in the way of progressive "ethical" standards. Any 1950's high school American history curriculum would have clearly pointed out that we are a country founded on law and that the United States has the only Constitution in world history constructed to limit the power of central government. In essence, the U.S. Constitution contains seemingly negative amendments that spell out what its central government cannot do, with inherent "checks and balances" afforded to the states and their respective representatives, which is clearly referred to in the Constitution as "We the People."

The first words of the preamble of the United States Constitution are, "We the People of the United States . . ." While the Preamble in which those words appear does not actually have any innate legal implications beyond introducing the rest of the Constitution, the meaning of the Preamble, with regard to the Constitution, is paramount towards understanding the intent of the Constitution.[130]

It is interesting to note that present day high school American History texts refer mainly to dates, events and a cursory understanding of an often revisionist version of American History. The objective of the progressive movement which President Obama represented, is to reach and re-educate the youth of this country, giving them a distorted view of the truth by playing on their emotions rather than facts. There is a difference between being tolerant to other countries' laws and customs and adopting them in preference to our own. Without historical records or accurate instruction from apolitical teachers and professors, the youth of our country will neither gain nor benefit from the collective wisdom and experience of our greatest generation. If historical events were taught as they actually occurred, one would recognize that the recruiting and indoctrinating the youth of this country would have a striking similarity to the recruiting and indoctrination of the youth during the reign of Nazi Germany;

---

[130] *http://constitution.laws.com/we-the-people*

placing President Obama's picture next to Adolph Hitler's pre-Nazi Germany. Surely President Obama had not been the sole architect of this strategy in the U.S. but his cavalier and often mesmerizing ability to distort truth without consequences, makes him a danger to the very survival of this country.

A sovereign country is defined by its borders, language and culture. President Obama's record on illegal immigration sometimes defies logic in the manner in which he enforced our country's Constitutional principles.

For example; try getting caught stepping one foot into a foreign country's borders like Costa Rica, Guatemala or Iraq, intentionally as an illegal immigrant, and you will be either shot on sight or imprisoned until the next ice age. Yet, some 13 million illegal immigrants have entered through this country's borders and were treated as a potential voting block for Obama's progressive agenda. What country would actually be considering amnesty as a way of making the illegal immigration issue go away? For this act alone, President Obama is the laughingstock of the world and a traitor to our constitutional laws.

Dan Bubalo is an expert in finance and an outspoken proponent of exposing the "intractable nature of government and its inextricable hold and influence on financial markets." He published a hard-hitting conservative commentary in the "Daily Rant" September 9, 2013, evaluating the Obama presidency. He stated "When Derek Jeter comes to bat for the New York Yankees during a televised game, enough statistics appear beneath his name to let viewers know everything but his shoesize. Batting average, batting average with runners in scoring position, playoff batting average, height, weight, years in the league, and fielding percentage, etc. That statistical flash is common to other sports as well, so I have a very basic question: why is that same statistical data-base not used every time a politician is looking for face-time and running their mouths during an interview?" Later, he writes,

"In 2007, then Senators Obama, Clinton, Kerry, Biden, McCain and Hagel all opposed President Bush's recommendations to imposing severe sanctions on Syria's Assad for human rights abuses. However, during Obama's presidency, they were in lockstep saying that our country must respond militarily under the War Act, attempting to do so because in some way Syria can threaten national security."[131]

The problem with Obama's administration and its "shuck and jive" routine, was that it successfully and repeatedly deflects attention away from its ineptitude. One had to pay close attention to what was playing out in Syria: amazingly, all the other scandals had almost magically disappeared. No more NSA, Snowden, IRS, Gun-Running, Eric Holder or Benghazi in the news. We no longer are discussing the economy, Obama care or the looming debt ceiling crisis. With the advent of digitized video, microphones and cell phones, it's almost impossible to lie about what one has said and yet, Obama proving to be pathological by nature, declaring he never talked about crossing the "red line" with reference to Syria, instead chastising the world as if it was their suggestion instead of his.

The massive taxation, euphemistically known as Obamacare, will deserve a closer look with reference to Obama's place in history. We didn't know how it will be administered, we didn't know how it will be accessed, we didn't know how the exchanges were to work once they are in fill effect, but we know for certain there are 16,000 new IRS agents, armed and ready to collect our money.

Obama is unique in that his demeanor on and off teleprompter speaks volumes. At the G-20 summit in September 2013, Obama was caught off teleprompter in an impromptu address to the delegates. He stammered until finally and incoherently he spoke about his creating jobs in America, almost as if in perpetual campaign mode. How does this relate to the focus of the most important international economic and financial issues facing

---

[131] *http://mychal-massie.com/premium/the-obama-presidency-in-a-nutshell*

the world? Amazing is Obama's lack of comprehension in the presence of true world leaders.

From a president who has no military strategic planning skills, it is lunacy to accept this president as credible. Informing an enemy that he's going to bomb their country in a couple weeks without a defined military objective as required by the War Powers Act,[132] potentially places the U.S. in imminent danger. All this while the world was watching and assessing. To other world leaders this must seem like a "B" rated movie just before intermission. Obama shamed this country and continued to do so daily on the international stage.

During a 2009 interview with George Stephanopoulos, President Obama said that he absolutely rejects the notion that the federal health care mandate is a tax increase. Remarkably, the Supreme Court, in a 5-4 ruling written by nominal conservative Chief Justice John Roberts, rejected the Obama administration's argument that the Constitution's Commerce Clause permits an individual health care mandate. The Court also claimed that it could impose such a directive by a direct un-apportioned tax, meaning Justice Roberts illogically approved the Healthcare Affordability Act as if it were an equal tax for everyone; which is not true. Constitutional scholars and former Supreme Justices unanimously state that any tax that would create highly unjust results on apportionment was not a direct tax. An apportioned income tax on people requires each person pay the same amount of tax. Chief Justice Roberts has made it constitutionally legal for the federal government to essentially force an individual to buy health insurance from the federal government whether they want to or not, making the tax issue an IRS offense for not doing so.[133]

On Circumventing Constitutional Law

During the 2008 campaign Obama positioned himself as a constitutional authority, standing up for the sovereignty and

---

[132] http://www.answers.com/topic/war-powers-act
[133] http://truthintaxation.us/?tax inform=universeTaxes

rights of the people. Back then, Obama chastised President George W. Bush's use of "signing statements" that the president issues when signing legislation. These are printed together with the legislation, but do not have the force of law. Yet, these "signing statements" are an attempt to undermine the exclusive legislative power of Congress. In 2008, Obama stated at a rally of enthusiastic supporters that he taught the Constitution for 10 years and believes in the Constitution and will obey the Constitution of the United States stating "we're not gonna use signing statements as a way to do an end-run around Congress." As President, not only did Obama adopted the use of signing statements but explicitly declared his intention to circumvent Congress on many occasions, including the State of the Union address in both 2012 and 2013, essentially stating "If Congress won't act . . . I will."[134]

Obama's 2014 State of the Union address was no different as to his contempt for the "rule of law", which states "The rule of law is a basic concern in the creation of the Constitution. Constitutional law can only be fully and effectively implemented when the laws of a country or region as a whole are respected by the citizenry and the Government."[135] No one in a free society is above the law, especially elected officials who are at the behest of the electorate. President Obama's message for the divided Congress (that largely stymied his agenda for three years) was that he didn't actually need congress; he's got a pen and he can use it to sign executive orders to move his agenda forward.[136]

Concern about signing statements seemed rather insignificant as the president was openly defying Congress. Obama's repeated refusal to enforce federal laws, including the employer mandate of Obamacare (his own signature achievement) violates Article II, Section 3 of the Constitution which states that the president "shall take Care that the Laws be faithfully executed." This is a duty, not a discretionary power. While the president does have

[134] http://www.whitehouse.gov/the-press-office/2012/01/24/remarks-president- state-union-address
[135] http://constitution.laws.com/rule-of-law
[136] http://nbcpolitics.nbcnews.com/ news/2014/01/26/22455927-frustratedobamas-message-ill-go-it-alone?lite&ocid=msnhp&pos=1

substantial discretion about how to enforce a law, he has no discretion about whether to do so.[137] Authoritarian or autocratic leadership is characterized by individual control over all decisions and little input from group members. This style of leadership typically makes choices based on their own ideas and judgments and rarely accepts advice from others. Autocratic leadership involves absolute, authoritarian control over a group.[138]

Congress is made up of elected officials representing the people. For a sitting president to berate congress for standing in his way of implementing programs diametrically opposed by the majority of the citizens of the country sounds dictatorial. Insisting on economic programs Congress determines is detrimental to the survival of the country, with disregard for the constitutional laws and protocols he swore to uphold, is the act of a tyrant.

On Immigration

President Obama has acted to circumvent the legislative process, providing illegal aliens with employment authorization. He and former Secretary of Homeland Security Janet Napolitano claim that this is nothing more than a matter of "prosecutorial discretion." Circumventing the law is not "prosecutorial discretion" but instead "prosecutorial deception." Many of the statements made by the President and by Secretary of Homeland Security Napolitano on immigration are often misleading fabrications of the truth. The President referred to the aliens who would benefit from his use of prosecutorial discretion as *dreamers*, an obvious reference to the DREAM Act. Obama stated that this legislation was not passed due to inaction by congressional politicians.[139]

The story is that Congressional politicians did act. They acted decisively to vote down both the DREAM Act and Comprehensive Immigration Reform; legislation that was, in the view of those elected representatives who voted against those bills, not in the

[137] http://www.breitbart.com/InstaBlog/2013/07/10/King-Obama-Violates- the-Constitution
[138] http://psychology.about.com/od/leadership/f/autocratic-leadership.htm
[139] http://latino.foxnews.com/latino/politics/2012/06/17/obama-invokesprosecutorial-discretion-to-circumvent-constitution-and-congress

best interests of our nation or our citizens. Under our Constitution, the Congress represents the will of the people. It appears that this administration was acting to circumvent the immigration laws that Congress would not amend or alter.

U.S. immigration laws provide a lawful means for lawful immigrants to acquire United States citizenship through the naturalization process, a process that both this author's grandparents proudly went through. These laws are not simply a formality but are intended to make certain that our nation does not simply hand out the "keys to the kingdom" that citizenship provides. The President stated that we are a nation of laws and a nation of immigrants. Yet by his actions, our immigration laws would be ignored and instead administered by the dictatorial whims of the Obama presidency.

On the Debt Ceiling

The raging debates that took place over the 2013 impasse over the raising of the debt ceiling were a prime example of the looming dictatorial grip Obama has over the destruction of our constitutional form of government. The debt ceiling is, by definition, the upper limit of borrowing allowed to the government. To argue over raising the debt ceiling is an oxymoron. Nonetheless, raising the debt ceiling, rather than taking the wisdom of Economics 101 or perhaps coming up with budgetary restraints, is occurring each time our debt is exceeded.

President Obama was personally and deliberately lying, by scaring the public into believing that our country will default if the debt ceiling isn't permanently raised. Obama had outright refused to negotiate any congressional proposal on the debt ceiling that is short of untethered expansion of borrowing. This insanity goes against Obama's constitutional obligation of protecting this country from economic default by all means.

Congressional law, in conjunction with the Secretary of the Treasury, states that economic default on the debt of the U.S. will never occur since it's the obligation of the Secretary of the Treasury and not the president, to ensure that as tax money comes into the Federal Reserve, paying the national debt comes first. Since Obama choses to force a debt ceiling crisis rather than attend to constitutional safeguards, he is in violation of his constitutional duties.

In an October 6, 2013 article in *The New Republic*, speculation was presented on ways Obama could act on his own to raise the debt ceiling without congressional approval. If congress chooses not to act on the debt ceiling, there are three ways Obama could raise the debt ceiling:

1. First, he could argue that, under the best reading of the relevant statutes, Congress has forced him to act unconstitutionally because he cannot literally comply with the debt ceiling, therefore ordering him to borrow rather than cut expenditures.

2. The president could argue that he must borrow money under Section 4 of the 14th Amendment, which provides that "The validity of the public debt of the United States, authorized by law . . . shall not be questioned." However, it is Congress, not the president that possesses the power to borrow under Article I of the Constitution; the 14th Amendment does not change that rule.

3. The president can declare an emergency and justify borrowing by citing reasons of national security and do so by invoking his "inherent" executive powers under Article II of the Constitution; something he has been doing regularly regardless of the true intent of the executive order.[140]

As it turned out, congress decided to cave into Obama's whims, effectively giving up their constitutional power to stop the madness of out of control spending and debt. The charade

[140] http://www.newrepublic.com/article/115034/debt-ceiling-3-ways-obama-could-circumvent-congress

of saving the country from a catastrophic economic collapse in the nick of time plays well in the press and with the ill-informed, yet it only proves that in Washington its business as usual. The Republican conservative base had stepped into a mine field by doing as they were elected to do. The Republican Party allowed another trillion dollars to be borrowed for one year, did not attempt to gain any ground in stopping Obamacare and basically agreed to compromise in one direction only. In doing so, it further proves that our two-party system is one party posing as two, with the conservatives from both sides of the aisle cast as enemies of the state (domestic terrorists) by instigating an attempt at a balanced U.S. economy.

About two weeks prior to the vote on the debt ceiling deadline, as Tea Party (conservatives) within the Republican-controlled House were attempting to enforce constitutional law, some House Democrats sent a private message to House Speaker John Boehner: "If you need to break with the die-hard conservatives of your caucus to keep the government running and avoid a debt ceiling crisis, we might be able to try to help you protect your speakership, should far-right Republicans rebel and challenge you."[141]

The result of Congress allowing the government to continue in the direction of physical and economic collapse, there is no longer any doubt that the die was cast allowing the "neutering" of Congress from its assigned duties under the constitution. The agreement, allowing "kicking the economic can" down the road another six months, now contains language allowing the automatic raising of the debt ceiling if Congress or the President fails to pass a bill to prevent it. This authorizes the Treasury to use "extraordinary measures" to pay bills without Congressional oversight by the House of Representatives, as required by the Constitution.[142] This unreported addition within the 2013 debt ceiling deal amounts to national suicide, leaving the "elites" untethered power. This is something Jefferson, Madison, Hamilton and other founding fathers of our country tried to protect us from.

---

[141] *http://www.motherjones.com/politics/2013/10/john-boehner-democrats- debt-ceiling-deal-speakership*
[142] *http://www.motherjones.com/mojo/2013/10/senate-reaches-deal-raise- debt-ceiling-and-end-shut-down*

After the 9/11 tragedies, Congressional decision makers once again overruled its own Constitutional obligations by conveniently inventing the term "extraordinary measures" to skirt the law by tossing away the 4th amendment. This was done in order to quickly adopt an unread Patriot Act, which provides the federal government vast powers to access personal information, perform search and seizures and detain suspects in the interest of national security - without due process or warrant.[143]

The 4th Amendment reads: "The right of the people to be secure in their persons, houses, papers, and effects, against unreasonable searches and seizures, shall not be violated, and no Warrants shall issue, but upon probable cause, supported by Oath or affirmation, and particularly describing the place to be searched, and the persons or things to be seized." Regrettably, the days when a presidential oath to "preserve, protect, and defend the Constitution of the United States" may be behind us, as leaders hide behind secret courts that literally emasculate the Constitution at will.

How an educated leader like Obama, professing to be a constitutional expert, could allow such constitutional destruction, really should not be that surprising. One must always filter the incredible and intentional decisions to bring this country to its knees, through the prism of Saul Alinsky's *Rules for Radicals*, of which this progressive government has seemed to adopt. The intentional and personal attacks on select House conservative Republicans as being radicals and enemies of this country for their part in the shutdown of the government and attempting the defunding of Obamacare is a perfect adaption of Rules 5 and 12:

RULE 5: "Ridicule is man's most potent weapon." "There is no defense. It's irrational. It's infuriating. It also works as a key pressure point to force the enemy into concessions."

---

[143] *http://m.gulfnews.com/opinion/how-to-destroy-the-us-constitution-1.1220322*

RULE 12: "Pick the target, freeze it, personalize it, and polarize it." "Cut off the support network and isolate the target from sympathy. Go after people and not institutions; people hurt faster than institutions."[144]

Obama again performed his oratory magic at the conclusion of the congressional debt ceiling charade by telling the American people that this new trillion-dollar borrowing does not go to our debt but is being used to pay our bills. To even consider his statement as credible is an embarrassment. Borrowing money to pay back interest on previously borrowed money is the definition of a financial collapse waiting to unfold. Seemingly, this was the ultimate objective of this progressive administration.

Obama's legacy will be that he is the first president that openly and successfully violated his constitutional obligations without punishment. These are impeachable acts let alone acts of sabotage. It must only be concluded, by the enormity of Obama's fundamental attempt at transforming this country, that he and the majority of congress are working together to rid this country of its constitution while forming ever closer ties to the dictatorial constructs of Socialism. Obama may not be the first or last president in the long chain of progressive-minded presidents since Woodrow Wilson, to move this country away from its founding principles but he will be the first president to achieve a quantum leap toward the destruction of this country.

Historically, following the economic collapse of foreign countries is not a topic taught in schools and will especially be avoided under Common Core education. The debt cycle is a complicated network of political and power-hardened financial corporations working clandestinely to suck the wealth out of the Gross Domestic Product (GDP) of a country, while funneling it into a larger, all-powerful, central government destined to "rule" over its population instead of governing. The beginning of the recent European debt cycle began in Spain. To recapture financial stability, Spain made the

[144] http://www.bestofbeck.com/wp/activism/saul-alinskys-12-rules-for-radicals

decision to sell its sovereign bonds at 6%, while the bond market, in general, was hovering near zero percent return. Other broke nations, banks and investment firms borrowed money from the European Central Bank (ECB) that administers to the European monetary policies at zero percent and bought Spanish bonds at 6%. This represents a massive loss to the ECB.

The ECB in turn printed Euros and bought sovereign bonds directly and in unlimited quantity from Spain; a catastrophic and illegal banking practice. As Spain sold more and more bonds, the debt to GDP ratio rose dramatically leading to hyperinflation, unemployment and a weakening economy. As the Spanish economy weakened, the Spanish government increased its debt ceiling even more calling it a "stimulus."

The population soon found out that it could not earn money and forced the government to do something. In response the Spanish government raised its debt ceiling to add more stimulus money into the economy. As Spain's economy weakened further, bank loans defaulted, and the "real" value of property plummeted. To give the illusion of sound property values, secured loans on real estate are booked as being worth far more than they actually are, and unsecured loans become unsalvageable. The entire banking system was revealed to be insolvent and a run on the banks began.

As financial risk increases, interest rates rise even further. As interest rates increased, Spain needed to borrow more money from the European Central Bank to service its sovereign debt and bail out banks. This means borrowing additional money just to pay off interest on prior loans. As Spain's economic picture spirals out of control, it becomes clear that their downward economic outlook is not about economics or proper management of money. This behavior is purely about political whoring, doing anything to maintain the power base.

The reality is that those in power are not knowledgeable about economics, yet the people have the perception that they are. Politicians are not economists; they are interested in power and control is often the reason that entire nations go bust. Politicians will remain in power and will see to it that public becomes responsible for the debt in the form of inflated taxes and outright confiscation of wealth via computer transfer of funds from the private sector to the "state."[145]

This scenario has played out in Greece and will soon be complete in Italy and is the very reason the U.S. is about to fall victim to the same debt spiral. Those in power use political correctness as the tool to subdue intelligence. Political correctness has allowed unqualified people to run the world. Intelligence must rise to the top and re-assert its dominance in the arena of political and economic stability. The public has been coerced into thinking that re-asserting intelligence for stupidity is racist. These are the principles of Saul Alinsky coming to fruition and are the very reason the Constitution was constructed as it is: to protect citizens from a corrupt central government.

Once out of control, there are no "political" solutions. Loss of power, due process in a court of law and extreme punishment are the only lasting solutions. So it was with the American Revolution, so it was in Biblical times where it was stated in the Book of Exodus that "the punishment shall be life for life, and eye for an eye and a tooth for a tooth." A corrupt government breeds lawlessness. This is where personal responsibility and the Rule of Law comes into play. Governing bodies have the responsibility of providing due process, where just punishment is provided for lawlessness. Without the public actively demanding compliance to the "law" anarchy is the result.[146] Once lawlessness takes hold of a society, that society is doomed to collapse

Allowing the debt cycle to take hold in the U.S. is exactly what happened to cause the collapse of the subprime mortgage market. Jon Corzine, the former governor of New Jersey and former CEO

[145] http://www.forbes.com/sites/billfrezza/2013/10/15/the-international-monetaryfund-lays-the-groundwork-for-global-wealth-confiscation
[146] http://en.wikipedia.org/wiki/Anarchy

of MF Global Holdings, Ltd., is a prime example of uncontrolled power gone badly. Corzine had built an empire working with other people's money as the chairman and senior partner of Goldman Sachs. As unsecured loans began to emerge, the financial industry underwriting guidelines began to loosen, as a way of stimulating economic growth. It was the duty of Corzine and others to recognize financial instability in the making but instead Corzine decided to "feed the economic beast," which included taking TARP (Troubled Asset Recovery Program) money from the US treasury to pay 953 Goldman Sacks employees bonuses of at least $1 million each, instead of implementing corrective financial measures to firm up the subprime mortgage debacle.[147] After receiving their bonuses many of the Goldman Sacks executives resigned and moved on into government positions.

Internationally, Goldman Sachs helped Greek government mask the true facts concerning its national debt between the years 1998 and 2009, eventually leading to the economic collapse of the Greek economy. Italy's former prime minister and finance minister became an international adviser to Goldman Sachs, resulting in the eminent collapse of the Italy's economy.

Stephen Friedman, a former director of Goldman Sachs, was named Chairman of the New York Federal Reserve Bank of in January 2008, while illegally continuing to own stock in Goldman Sachs. Goldman Sachs conversion from a securities firm to a bank holding company in September 2008, meant it was now regulated by Stephen Friedman of the Federal Reserve and not the Security and Exchange Commission.

Timothy Geithner, as president of the New York Federal Reserve from 2003 to 2009, was arrested by the NYPD for his role in encouraging AIG (American International Group) from publicly disclosing payouts to banks to cover bad loans with taxpayer money.[148] Instead of jail time, Geithner was promoted to US Treasury Secretary in 2009 by President Barack Obama.

[147] http://scottskyrm.com/2013/04/mistakes-made-by-jon-corzine-and-mf-global
[148] http://www.opednews.com/articles/Timothy-Geithner-To-Resign-by-AbigailW-Adams-121228-397.html

On Terrorism

When President Obama signed the 2012 National Defense Authorization Act (NDAA), he allowed the military detention of American citizens without charge (section 1021). This essentially aims to put the last nail in the coffin of our Constitution and our most basic democratic traditions.

"President Obama's action today is a blight on his legacy because he will forever be known as the president who signed indefinite detention without charge or trial into law," said Anthony D. Romero, ACLU executive director. "The statute is particularly dangerous because it has no temporal or geographic limitations and can be used by this and future presidents to militarily detain people captured far from any battlefield."[149]

Under the legislation, suspects can be held without trial until the end of hostilities. They will have the right to appear once a year before a committee that will decide if the detention will continue. Further, it wasn't asked for by any of the agencies in the fight against terrorism in the United States. It breaks with over 200 years of tradition in America against using the military in domestic affairs. In fact, the heads of several security agencies, including the FBI, CIA, the director of national intelligence and the attorney general objected to the legislation. However, the corporate elite who drive the disastrous and inhumane polices of this country see it otherwise, and they, not the generals or anyone else, call the shots! A persistent counterinsurgency directed against the American people is about more than social control. It amounts to a direct attack on the person, an unreasonable search and seizure and the suppression of popular resistance, dissent and protest. All of that is recast as civil disorder, civil disturbance and domestic terror with consequences that include death.

Current U.S. military preparations for suppressing civil disturbance and domestic terrorism include the training of

---

[149] *http://www.informationclearinghouse.info/article30125.htm*

National Guard troops, local police and the authorization of massive surveillance.[150] Generally, these measures are in place to remove American freedoms.

To truly understand the scope of this sweeping legislation (National Defense Authorization Act), one must fully realize that the federal government is talking about American soil! This new edict states that law enforcement as well as military intelligence can order the killing of American citizens, if they are suspected to be terrorists or suspected of subversive activity against the U.S. In fact, this concept was taken directly from the Nazi government playbook, to protect the homeland. Where do you think the term Homeland Security came from? What the elitists are not stating is: who determines who is a terrorist? What is considered a terrorist activity? This is a direct assault against due process.

As a Senator, Obama claimed George W. Bush was a war criminal for questioning Americans with known ties to subversives because of lack of due process. He also wanted Bush impeached for enhanced interrogation techniques at Gitmo and vowed to close Gitmo within months of his first election.

As President, Obama wanted all terrorists at Gitmo to have Miranda Rights and be tried in civil courts to ensure due process, yet he has authorized the indefinite and, if need be, the killing of Americans in any location, without due process and without any representation at all by any court. In other words, Americans are now targets of their own government, without protection of the judicial system, without need for formal charges and can be killed for literally anything that the federal government might conceive of as terrorism. By the way, the term 'terrorism' has no formal meaning in terms of criteria. Elements of the military or federal government can act as judge and jury against American citizens, whereas formal terrorists in Gitmo are allowed due process and civil representation.

---

[150] *http://beforeitsnews.com/military/2013/05/the-american-military-coup-of2012%E2%80%B3-encroachment-upon-basic-free-doms-militarized-policestate-in-america-2452514.html*

Although the Constitution of the U.S. designated the President as the commander in chief of the armed forces, it is not a requirement to have military experience. Of our 43 presidents that have been sworn into office all but four have had some form of military training and experience. President Obama has had virtually no military training or experience. Obama had numerous foreign policy challenges during his presidency, specifically in dealing with Israel, Russia, China, Syria, Lebanon and Egypt. The results of Obama's attempts to "orate" solutions to world issues has lacked substance and follow through, lessening America's credibility. Foreign leaders have lost respect for American promises and leadership. Obama's image had been overmatched by events that somehow seem to worsen over time.

The ultimate firestorm created by Obama releasing five of the most prominent Taliban terrorists held in Guantanamo, in exchange for the release of Sgt. Bowe Bergdahl, simply defies the imagination. This is because he did this without giving 30 days' notice to Congress or the intelligence community, as required by the Constitution. Sgt. Bergdahl had made it known that he had no respect for the US military or America and was willing to denounce his citizenship and deserted his active duty company in Afghanistan, to start a new life. The army sent out a squadron to find Sgt. Bergdahl. In the attempt six US servicemen were killed by the Taliban, not knowing that Berghahl was captured and held hostage by the Taliban.[151]

The art of political negotiation is a delicate game of wills vs. strengths, where both parties must gain some advantage. Negotiating with terrorists, however, is a dangerous game punishable by more US soldiers being taken as trade for captured terrorists. Without a strategic advantage gained from the negotiations, the entire process has no purpose. Obama abandoned the US policy of never negotiating with terrorists to gain the release of a deserter who wanted no part of America. As a calculated, constitutionally illegal move by the president, how

---

[151] *http://www.washingtonpost.com/blogs/the-fix/wp/2014/06/01/sunday-showsrepublicans-blast-decision-to-trade-taliban-members-for-sgt-bergdahl*

does this compute as being in the best interest of our country? By all accounts Obama's temperament and experience, based on skill set and ability, is much better equipped as a community organizer than to be president of the United States.

On Public Respect

President Obama's ability to simply make up constitutional scenarios and stories as he goes along is now part of the public record. Off teleprompter, the real Obama shines through loud and clear. Having the bully pulpit was a huge advantage for Obama, allowing him say as he wishes knowing his critics will spend most of their time amplifying or discrediting his statements. Nonetheless Obama is reaching the general public that is unprepared to "fact check." It is most difficult to offer an offense when the American public gets a daily dose of mistruths.

During the government shutdown in 2013, President Obama had many options in terms of how much pain and suffering he wished to inflict on the population along with the usual political saber rattling. Obama chose to take a page from the teachings of Saul Alinsky by "never letting a good crisis go to waste." Obama realized that even after weeks of a government shutdown, nothing much was happening to force the anger in the American people necessary for him to offer additional government help (control). When political agendas become the main focus in government instead of national interests, mistakes are made that cut through the veneer of public perception. It is the job of every American citizen to learn from these mistakes. It is as C.S. Lewis says, "Experience is the cruelest, most merciless teacher, but it guarantees that you will learn."

The most insensitive act of disrespect against American citizens occurred when Obama closed The National Mall in Washington, D.C. due to lack of money. The National Mall is a two-mile stretch of land around the Capital. Visitors to The Mall find tree lined boulevards with historical monuments and memorials, world-famous museums and impressive federal buildings, all along Constitution Avenue. The National Mall welcomes millions of visitors every year, but it has also played host to many history-making events. This is where Martin Luther King, Jr. delivered his "I Have a Dream" speech to hundreds of thousands who marched on Washington. This is where protestors from those opposing the Vietnam War during the 1960s to the peaceful protests of the 1980s, to modern-day marchers rallying for and against everything from reproductive rights to big business, make their voices heard.

President Obama demonstrated massive indiscretion when he ordered The National Mall was closed to all U.S. veterans and citizens. Yet, Obama allowed the Federal government to issue a permit for thousands of illegal aliens to use The National Mall to protest for amnesty for illegal aliens, which suggests a kind of warped priority on behalf of the administration; one that cost him respect in the eyes of the public. However, it was Susana Flores, a spokeswoman for the illegal immigrant group that added further insult to our veterans and U.S. citizens by stating: "the National Park Service allowed us to have this rally because it is part of the First Amendment of the Constitution."[152]

It's not that Obama was a bad president; it is that he was a fraud posing as president. He has intentionally deceived a trusting U.S. population by using his oratory skills, charisma and apparent family values. He came from nowhere, with little apparent political baggage and had protection from the usual vetting process all potential presidents must go through. His political career was sketchy at best with no major senatorial contributions. His private life consisted of virtually no business or work experiences other than an apparent part time professorship and success as a community organizer. He never served in the armed forces, never had any military training or corporate experience necessary to understand the complexities of the highest office in the land.

---

[152] *http://www.foxnews.com/on-air/special-report-bret-baier/blog/2013/10/09/ thousands-gather-%E2%80%98closed%E2%80%99-na-tional-mallimmigration-reform-rally*

His private life and upbringing is a mystery along with his official transcripts and birth certificate. Even after his first election, it couldn't be proven Obama was even an American citizen until some copy of a birth certificate showed up not knowing if it was real or created. Obama's ties to subversives like Bill Aires & Bernadine Dohrn, who bombed the pentagon as members of the Weather Underground are sketchy, yet it seems all look the other way. He had ties to Cass Sunstein, who was appointed to serve on the National Security Administration's advisory panel after Sunstein openly supported untethered government surveillance of the private lives of conspiracy group. Sunstein has recognized the Muslim Brotherhood and some 41 personal associations with known radicals, some of which actually have clearance as government employees. So protected was this president (by the media) from any past or present occurrences that would hurt his approval ratings, that one would think he is a king. Yet public polling, after 5 years in office puts his approval rating at 37%. When the numbers do not add up to the deeds, the real conspiracy has yet to surface.

On Public Trust

Most Americans understand that politicians, right up to the president of the U.S., often lie with impunity. So rampant has this trend become that public trust hangs in the balance. The public wants to trust its elected officials but does little to hold them accountable. Voting has become a popularity contest where fundraising is taken more seriously than substance. In the visual world of social media, elections are won or lost by rhetoric.

President Obama, in his first term, laid out an aggressive plan of political transparency guided by constitutional law. He singled out the closing of "Gitmo," ending unpopular wars, bringing the world's leading terrorist to justice, lower education costs, making healthcare costs affordable to all Americans and lowering the federal deficit. Candidate Obama made some 24 distinct promises that catered to every voter. The result was a larger than life image of a man that "sent tingles down the leg" of seasoned reporting journalists Chris Mathews prior to the 2008 elections.

Obama's first term ended with the realization that virtually none of his pre-election promises came to pass, leaving some to rip into Obama's first term record. On Chris Matthews' May 15, 2013 commentary on *Hard Ball* Matthews realizes that "President Obama obviously likes giving speeches more than he does running the executive branch."[153]

As the saying goes: *Fool me once, shame on you; fool me twice, shame on me.* Despite Obama's obvious shortcomings, he was elected to a second term. Instead of bringing this country to a more solvent base, Obama raised the federal debt to 16 trillion dollars. More disturbing is that Obama has outright lied to the public and has little to no regard for the constitutional law he swore to uphold.

Presidential lying is not new, if so, why do we tolerate lying by high level public officials? Do these sound familiar? "I did not have sexual relations with that woman." "The Benghazi attack was the result of a demonstration against a video." "You can keep your doctor and your health plan."

President Lyndon Johnson lied about American ships being attacked at the Gulf of Tonkin, leading the U.S. into an 11-year war in Vietnam and more than 58,000 Americans killed in action. We were lied to by presidents Nixon, both Bushes and Clinton, and yet in the end, their only punishments are satires on *Saturday Night Live*. It is as if it's no big deal; all presidents lie. We should demand outrage for breach of public trust, let alone holding lying presidents accountable to the same laws "We the People" must abide.

---

[153] *http://www.politico.com/blogs/media/2013/05/chris-matthews-sours-onobama-164095.html*

Presidential lying has become part of pre-election banter. During the 2012 re-election campaign of President Obama, he stated that "we've got al-Qaida on its heels." This may have been good pre-election hype, but U.S. military commanders and intelligence agencies knew otherwise. Al-Qaida was stronger than ever, making Obama untrustworthy.[154] President Obama telling the American public that they could keep their doctors and health plans some 27 times in the media in order to get this program passed, was an outright lie leaving millions of people suffering today because of it

Lies violate the oath of office to "preserve, protect and defend" the Constitution. President Obama not only lied but approves of liars among his top staff. Susan Rice was rewarded with a promotion for lying to America about Benghazi. National Intelligence Director James Clapper lied to Congress about not collecting records on individual Americans. Attorney General Eric Holder lied to Congress about gun running to Mexican cartel criminals in the "Fast and Furious" scandal as well as lying to congress about approving warrants to search the records of Fox News reporter James Rosen.

If any politician elected with the full trust and backing of the American people, openly lies to the American people, his or her credibility is lost, and that person cannot be trusted. The issue of lying by any government official warrants judges to step in and remove the offenders. However, Federal and Supreme Court judges who are appointed by a standing president, are not about to excoriate the executor and chief. The result is a lasting stain on the nation. This issue is not about party politics. It warrants punishment and not executive orders. Until law and order is restored at the highest political levels, criminal activity will flourish, challenging national security and our very way of life.

---

[154] http://www.floridatoday.com/article/20140117/COLUMNISTS0205/301170002/Guest-column-Presidential-lies

For Further Reading

"A List of Goldman Sachs People in the Obama Government: Names Attached to the Giant Squid's Tentacles | MyFDL." fflambeaus myFDL diary Site Wide Activity RSS. http://my.fireoglake.com/fflambeau/2010/04/27/a-list-of-goldman-sachs-people-in-the-obama-government-names-attached-to-the-giant-squids-tentacles/ (accessed July 21, 2014).

"Obama's Promises: Scorekeeping the First Term." http://www.stamfordadvocate.com/local/article/Obama-s-promises-Scorekeeping-the-first-term-4210008.php#page-3 (accessed July 21, 2014).

EPILOGUE

The inspiration to write this book was influenced by the writings of Ayn Rand and her unique insights into American politics. Her metaphors, based on her oppressive upbringing under the Marxist Russian government of the early 1900's, set the stage for an American renaissance some 50 years after her writings. Sadly, the political and educational pendulum is shifting away from the concepts of individual rights and freedoms and back towards the roots of Socialism, Marxism and Progressive ideologies. President Obama is the most recent pawn of the Socialist movement within this country. His abuse of executive powers, without apparent restraint or resistance by congress, is a sure indicator that our Constitution has been bastardized. No longer do we have the checks and balances of "separation of powers" but instead have one political party posing as two. Citizens are easily pacified with the illusion of control, making it easier to implement the platform of the total progressive transformation of the American way of life.

A glimmer of hope resides in the tenacity of those still able to think outside the restraints of entitlements. They are a small but growing force, presently embodied in the formation of the Tea Party and the likes of young senators and representatives as well as the emergence of conservative talk radio. All of these people are giving voice to the resistance while putting their careers on the line, as did our founding fathers. The question is: do we have enough time and educational expertise to keep the American dream alive? The ultimate litmus test will be if "We the People" can recognize its inherent Constitutional power and not be fooled by the unsubstantiated progressive rhetoric that over promises and under delivers.

This country was founded on principles that served as a directive for the Constitution of the United States. The brave souls that dared to challenge the oppressive, established norms of Europe did so with the intent of placing the power and responsibility of self-determination into the hands of the people. Surely there needs to be common rules and guidelines to follow in order to ensure stability and equal opportunity under the laws of the land. In every culture, tribe or animal species, there is *order*. That order requires guidelines of enforcement by a leader, chieftain or alpha male. The United States is a grouping of individual states encompassing a variety of cultural differences that voluntarily agreed to abide by a Constitution. We talk of founding principles as if they were facts necessary to study for a "pop quiz." A closer analysis reveals that these principles were mere statements of common beliefs required for a free society. All rights come from God, not government; meaning that all men are created equal under the creator. ***All political power is derived from the people*** which was embodied in the first three words of the constitution: "We the People." A direct democracy can lead to mob rule; therefore the principle of a ***limited representative republic*** protected the people from an oppressive government. A ***written constitution*** is a contract among the states, necessary to ensure unity as well as a guide for security against interpretation by a centralized government. Finally, there had to be ***private property rights***, which is the hallmark of a free society; not just property but the right itself.

The Constitution of the United States is not a limitation on individual freedoms but a security against a controlling centralized government. There needs to be a leader that acts as the executor of the State, along with representatives from the individual states whose job it is to insure the voice of the people is heeded. Together, this representative government is the voice of the people, giving specific direction to the Executive as well as the Legislative and Judicial branches of government, to carry out the daily administration tasks of the state.

The reason why monarchs last is that people lose interest in the actions of the state, relinquishing their "rights" by default in the hope of benevolence. To move from our founding principles to the present state of executive lawlessness, required the one element not anticipated by our founding fathers: the diligence of the people. It has been said that no democracy survives more than 200 years, the time it takes for individual complacency to override responsibility. We must think hard and remain vigilant to the insidious transformation of America, as promised by then-candidate Obama. You can't transform America without changing America. The difference between a monarch and a president can be nothing more than *We the People* relinquishing personal freedoms. One thing is for sure, once freedom is lost, it will take another American Revolution to start anew.

Dr. Sal Martingano

salmartingano.com

a "R.V" heard",)
saw him on T.V,)
but does)
not accept "some" of
his views)

near Dallas!!!